HIGH MAINTENANCE WOMEN

First published 2023

All inquiries should be made to the publishers.

Big Sky Publishing Pty Ltd
PO Box 303, Newport, NSW 2106, Australia
Phone: 1300 364 611
Fax: (61 2) 9918 2396
Email: info@bigskypublishing.com.au
Web: www.bigskypublishing.com.au

Cover design and typesetting: Think Productions

A catalogue record for this book is available from the National Library of Australia

Title: High Maintenance Women
ISBN: 9781922896162

Printed and bound in Australia by Griffin Press

HIGH MAINTENANCE WOMEN

LISA PORTOLAN

This is an intelligent read and so wonderful to hear someone speaking on dating apps in such a refreshing and real tone. Reflects the reality of dating apps without the sensational gloss you see in the media - and reminds us to stand up and reclaim our power. This is a much-needed, real discussion about love and relationships in Australia.

Alita Bryon the founder of Bad Dates of Melbourne (BDOM)

Lisa does an excellent job of delving into the complex (and frustrating) world of dating, confused men and strong women. Having been labelled 'intimidating' by more men that I can remember, this book struck a chord!

Amanda Goff (Samantha X)

Contents

1

Uber findings

It's not often that you slide into a BMW X5 Uber. On a high from a television gig, I liked that the car seemed to match the tone of the morning. I rarely did TV interviews, and they still made me feel giddily successful – a rare occurrence for a PhD researcher.

'Paddington?' the Uber driver asked me in a nonchalant, this-is-my-twentieth-Uber-trip-this-morning kind of a tone.

I nodded emphatically. Even his indifferent air couldn't shake my post-TV euphoria.

As we stopped at the traffic lights in Pyrmont he said, 'Were you just on TV?'

He glanced at me in the rear-view mirror, assessing me impassively from behind his gaudy gold aviators. They looked expensive. Like the car.

'Yeah.'

'I pick up guests from the show all the time.'

'Figures.'

He had picked me up from the collection bay at *Studio 10*. It was hardly surprising.

The lights changed and he accelerated. I was hoping for a quiet trip. I had some thinking to do. I liked to mentally replay TV interviews. The questions they had asked and my responses. Carefully unpicking the details. Making sure I had been factual, relaxed, amenable, even. This was a process which I undertook after every TV interview, and it might last for an hour, days, maybe even weeks. A clear sign that I was an amateur.

'What did you, you know, talk about?' His manner was still blasé but his questions betrayed his interest.

'I talked about my research,' I responded. A topline kind of reply. A subtle indicator that I wasn't interested in continuing the conversation. I was too preoccupied by my personal assessment to chat. Let me indulge in a moment of narcissism already!

He didn't get the message.

'You're a researcher, then? An academic?'

'Something like that,' I said, unwilling to give away my status as a lowly PhD researcher.

'What do you research?'

Here's the catch. I had learnt very early along in my PhD journey not to tell anyone what my research topic was – it tended to open a Pandora's box of personal anecdotes. Unfortunately, I sensed there was no squirming out of this discussion. Mr Indifferent was also Mr Persistent.

'I research dating apps and intimacy.'

'Really?' His dispassionate persona was shaken.

This was kind of standard when people discovered my academic discipline. The reason? Most people have used a dating app – and most people have something to say about their experience.

'Yes, I look at whether dating apps change the way relationships are navigated, whether they change intimacy, and whether they reinforce gender stereotypes.'

'And what are your findings?'

Internally, I screamed. It wasn't that easy. I didn't have

a bullet list of findings that I could easily rattle off. People were complicated, messy, contradictory – especially when it came to their intimate lives. Generally, the person asking the questions wanted a sound bite – and intimacy just didn't work that way.

'Hmmmm,' I murmured. 'It's not so easy to summarise.'

'I see. People are … complicated.'

They were indeed. Even though I didn't want to hear his personal story, *I did at the same time.*

'Do you use dating apps?' I vomited out, unable to keep the snoop in me at bay.

'Yeah, yeah, of course. Doesn't everyone? I mean, I'm in a relationship now, but before that I used Tinder all the time.'

Like I said – everyone has a story to tell, from the mundane to the extravagantly explicit.

'I dated a lot of girls from apps.'

'Oh, yeah, and what was that like for you?' I found myself asking, slipping into researcher mode, despite the changed context.

'Honestly?' Long pause. 'There were a lot of gold-diggers.'

'Gold-diggers?' I managed. Now here was a new term. Or a recycled one. I hadn't heard about gold-diggers since *Dynasty*, shoulder pads and the 1980s.

'Yeah, you know, like, high maintenance girls.'

Now that term I had heard. A lot. During my research. It had never occurred to me that the high maintenance girl might be the updated version of the gold-digger.

'I used to work in finance, hedge fund sort of stuff…'

That explained the car…

'I lost my job during Covid and decided to pick up Uber driving, you know, to give me something to do.'

I did know. Covid had been unkind to many of us, and being a serial city Uber commuter, I had come across my fair share of Uber-driving Covid casualties.

I nodded.

'But before then…I was always dating these high maintenance girls. The ones that make you pay for dinner… And everything else!' He chortled, expecting me to join in with the laughter. This happened a lot. Men always think you will be quick to criticise other women. He had misread the room (or car in this case).

'And could you tell these girls were high maintenance from their dating app profiles?' I asked, unable to stop the sociological questioning flow.

'Kind of.'

'How?'

'Well, they're super-done-up in their profile shots. Lots of makeup, lots of work, expensive clothes… All the photos are taken on the party scene.'

'But you would still go on a date with them?' I asked.

'Yeah, well, they were hot. Do you blame me?'

Yes. Yes, I did blame him. But now was not the time to mention it.

'You know what's a dead giveaway?'

I didn't, but I suspected he would tell me anyway.

'When you're at the restaurant with them, and you spot that they have a Louis Vuitton or Prada handbag or something, and then at some point they pull out their wallet and it's a matching Louis Vuitton or Prada – like, *it's a set* – that's a clear sign that they're high maintenance.'

I found myself inadvertently tucking my peach Prada (which I had bought myself, with my own money!) out of sight.

'So, what would you do at that point? You've seen the bag and wallet, you know she's high maintenance, what do you do next?'

'Pay the bill and get the fuck out. And block her number. If you have it.'

Seemed logical. Insert eye-roll.

'But what if she *just* liked an expensive handbag? How is that conclusive proof that she's high maintenance?' I demanded, suddenly emotionally invested. It was becoming apparent that women were *first* told they needed the designer handbag, *and then* told they were gold-diggers for carrying it!

'It is, trust me. It is conclusive proof that they're high maintenance. Don't get me wrong – they're good-looking girls, but they want your money. They want everything … they're just *too* much. You've got to get out fast before you get entangled.'

As usual, when I came across these sentiments, I was quietly horrified, but I maintained my dignified, researcher demeanour. (When they tell you that researchers are objective in field, they're lying. Researchers are human beings. And highly subjective.)

'Listen, do you know Abraham Maslow?'

'Yes, yes,' I said impatiently. Everyone's favourite theorist. 'Hierarchy of human needs,' I paraphrased.

'Yeah, so at the bottom is survival, getting by, then when that's satisfied, people move onto other needs like emotional and intellectual ones. These girls, the gold-diggers, they're stuck down the bottom, they're just looking to survive. You can't blame them. They need someone to pay for their lifestyle.'

Dear God, apparently it could get worse.

We were at the back of Paddington now. Near the Fiveways. I willed us forward, propelling us mentally onto Oxford Street where I lived.

'But I *did* meet my girlfriend on Tinder.'

I gritted my teeth.

'I see … and she's not high maintenance?'

'No, she's super, super-chill.'

'Great, good for you.' I tossed some words out like confetti at a wedding, eagerly awaiting the end of this distasteful trip.

'Yeah, she's a model you know, but super-low-maintenance.'

Far, far worse.

'How wonderful for you,' I said.

'Yeah, we're going up to the Whitsundays on the weekend. Staying on a friend's yacht.'

'Sounds lovely.'

As we pulled onto Oxford Street and he released me from that steel trap, it occurred to me that, somehow, he had done me a favour. *He* had managed to summarise my key findings in a short Uber ride.

High maintenance girls/women were despised.

They wanted too much.

This was both fiscal and emotional.

Heterosexual women needed to present themselves as effortlessly gorgeous (models, even), but ice-cube-chill.

They needed to be … 'cool girls'.

The patriarchy was alive and well – and critical to love and intimacy.

Post-TV interview serendipitous vibe decidedly killed.

Inside I dreamed of the death of the cool girl.

2

The high maintenance woman

Gillian Flynn's definition of the 'cool girl' in her best-selling book *Gone Girl* (later developed into a feature film) resonated with women world-wide. The cool girl is *relaxed*, and not interested in emotional drama. She is willing to have casual sex. Eats everything and always remains pencil thin (because we criticise women who try to strategically lose weight by dieting – case in point, Kim Kardashian and the tomato-sauna saga of 2022); she is naturally beautiful (no work required to maintain that appearance!); she is sexually explorative; she is wild; but, most importantly, she continues to love her man and makes few demands of him. And, of course, forgives her man for any wrongdoing.

Rom-coms, TV series and books have described and celebrated the 'cool girl' for decades – from *Serena Van der Woodson* on *Gossip Girl*, to *Andie* in *How to Lose a Guy in 10 Days*. The cool girl is a well understood, and rarely criticised, cultural identity.

Flynn's definition was revolutionary. Not only did she perfectly delineate the parameters of the cool girl but she also called her out. She *identified* her. The cool girl had evolved unchecked. A perfect example of embodied patriarchy. So carefully concealed that nobody seemed to think there was a problem with her.

Instead, we (and I mean, women) tried to emulate her. And men, they sought her out.

Many women seeking relationships, or intimacy, in the 1990s and 2000s have sought to embody the cool girl. And, I would argue, still do today.

Be the cool girl and get the guy. It's basically a bumper sticker.

My Uber driver packaged the cool girl neatly as the 'relaxed model'.

What is directly opposed to the effigy of the cool girl?

The high maintenance woman.

The term 'high maintenance' is part of everyday speech, and usually refers to a woman who places a high value on her personal image, wants or needs. Often uttered within the context of dating, the implication is that the woman in question is too much hard work; an easier, more relatable mate would be preferred.

Rarely, if ever, do we come across the term 'high maintenance man'.

My research relates to gender and intimacy on dating apps. I examine if dating apps change intimacy, how so, what type of relationships dating apps produce, and how gender is reproduced on dating apps.

On dating apps, users make split-second decisions, relying on profile pictures to guide them.

In my research into dating apps and heterosexual matches, I found that men seek to portray themselves as handsome, muscular – *tanned*, even – in their profile shots to attract more matches. Of course, there is an implied whiteness here, a kind of quiet sexual racism common on dating apps, and more broadly in Western society, which I explore later in this book in Chapter 13.

Conversely, women seek to portray themselves *against* a cultural idea. Women look to develop profiles which convey them as 'not high maintenance'.

'High maintenance' is a slippery and yet sticky category defined by physical and behavioural characteristics.

In her profile photos, the high maintenance 'girl' (as she was often described by the men and women in my research) was likely wearing 'too much' makeup and/or form-fitting clothes. She would be dressed for a party (or 'going out'). She would be pouting at the camera Instagram-style, or toting an expensive handbag.

Once tarnished with the high maintenance brush it was difficult to be perceived as otherwise.

Behaviourally, she was perceived as difficult. She wanted *things*, and expected a high standard. There was labour involved in dating her and therefore a financial burden.

As one male participant indicated:

> *There are plenty of super-attractive girls on dating apps [...] but I mean, I can't afford that sort of thing. It's too high maintenance.*

Women within my research sought to present themselves

as ‘pretty’ but ‘relatable’. They didn’t want to ‘intimidate’ a potential match through their images and behaviour.

As one female participant indicated, a high maintenance woman comes across as expecting too much. Instead, a woman’s profile should portray a kind of effortless, relaxed prettiness:

> *My everyday look is an oversized tee and very comfy clothes, but on my profile there’s the festival picture where I’m obviously done up and there are two other photos where I’m with friends […] I did feel the pressure where you should at least look pretty, but at the same time you need to look relatable. So, I guess at the same time, people aren’t intimidated to approach you.*
>
> *There is that pressure that you need to look friendly enough, but pretty enough, but not too friendly at the same time. It’s a weird line.*

This kind of identity management is nothing new, particularly on social media. It is distinctly pervasive for girls and young women who are generally represented as having (or being) too little or too much. Too fat or too thin; too clever or too stupid; too free or too restricted.

Here, the line was between sexiness and effortlessness. Female participants felt the urge to look pretty but also not so pretty that they might scare prospective matches off. Physical attributes, or ways of presenting oneself, were also often conflated with personal behaviours and expectations.

In effect, women had to portray themselves as naturally pretty, capable, expectation-less, fun-loving and, most importantly, easy-going, all to ensure a man's comfort.

Online, there are a multitude of ways women must rein themselves in to appease men: not complaining, not demanding too much, not expressing their needs, not having expectations for emotional openness or fulfilment.

In effect, not making any of the demands which are the necessary requirements for an intimate relationship based on equality and mutuality.

Ultimately, the 'high maintenance woman' was too much to handle – which confirmed known stereotypes that women are expected to be quiet, subservient, opinion-less, and always amenable. That they shouldn't be difficult or demanding.

It confirmed feminine mainstays that a woman is required to smile and make nice, not be too overt, and not take up too much space.

A certain invisibility was required, even in an online dating space.

In my research, the high maintenance woman came up time and time again, evoked by both men and women. It was done with such ease that it was difficult to identify what exactly about her made us all feel uncomfortable.

In this book, I describe *who* the high maintenance woman is, how she interacts with modern expectations and appearance management, the financial and emotional labour associated (which are somehow entangled), and the need for her invisibility not just on social media but more broadly in society.

I explain my research, how data was collected, some of the leading theorists that guided my work, and the social context in which this research was collated. This book is unapologetically non-linear. It focuses on case studies and anecdotes to tell the story (interviewees' quotes have been edited for clarity), and relies on the reader to make their own assessment. People are complex, contradictory and messy. They don't fit into neat boxes, and they don't follow arrow straight plot lines.

The 'high maintenance woman' I discovered defies expectations. At first glance, she appears to be the antithesis to any feminist movement: a woman shaped purely by the male gaze, physically enhanced (cleavage-rich and fish-lipped, influenced by the pornification of female attractiveness). She wears clothes that enhance her physical assets and she lives an Instagram-lensed lifestyle. Yet, at the same time, she demands things, she seeks emotional fulfilment on her terms, she is highly visible in all spaces … she is powerful. The high maintenance woman emerged as a new-age feminist.

Conversely, the 'cool girl' sagged – she was quiet, subservient and willing to go along with her man at her own peril.

Sadly, there was little space in between for women, only continued criticism and judgement.

The way women must negotiate how they're perceived reminds me of a trapeze artist walking a tightrope, hundreds of metres up in the sky – with no end in sight.

Destined to fall.

3

Amelia: Trapped somewhere between the cool girl and high maintenance

Amelia is one of my research case studies. She is 21 years old, studies media at university in the evenings and works full-time at an insurance company. She lives in an apartment in Redfern with a flatmate. She has a tight-knit circle of friends she has known since childhood, and she is looking for a connection.

She's not looking for love per se – she's looking for a *connection.*

Whether that be friendship, or sex, or a relationship. She

wants to *feel something* within the intimacy space.

She uses multiple apps (on and off) to meet with people, including Tinder, Bumble and Hinge.

'I would definitely prefer to meet people In Real Life, but people don't go out to meet *people* anymore. Like, you don't go to out to meet *someone*. If you go to a bar in town with friends, everyone there is just on a dating app, swiping. People just don't approach you anymore. Or they don't approach people like me. Maybe if you looked like Jennifer Lopez they would, but not someone like me.'

'What do you mean by "someone like you"?'

'You know … I'm not your typical good-looking girl. I'm kind of big, and I'm not that pretty.'

'Do you think men your age are more likely to go after stereotypically pretty women?'

'Yeah, of course. They might say they want someone more chill or relaxed, but really if they must choose between the good-looking girls and me, who are they going to go with? Not me, of course.' She laughs, seemingly comfortable (and uncomfortable) with this outcome.

'So, tell me a bit about your profile.'

'Well, it's a mixture of photos of me at festivals and doing stuff, out with friends. I like music, so I want to get across that it's important to me. I guess I want to show that I do *stuff*, I'm not the kind of girl that's just doing her makeup and buying clothes or whatever, there's more to me.'

'And do you feel like the images you've chosen are accurate – do they describe you well?'

'Yeah, most of them show my best side, you know? I'm not always dressed up and going to a festival. My average look is a long T-shirt and jeans, but I'm not going to put those sorts of images up, right? You have to sell it a bit.'

'Okay, and what's your bio like?'

'Oh, the bio is the hardest part. I get nervous writing my bio, so I usually get my friends to write it for me. Something funny and offbeat, because I'm kind of quirky.'

'You trust your friends with that?'

'Yeah, more than myself!'

'And do you have a fair bit of success – have you made some connections?'

'Yeah, I guess. Last year I met a guy online on Tinder. He was this skater, musician-type guy. My age. We started chatting online, and we talked for ages. We were constantly texting and sending each other memes and news stories and stuff. He was into music and festivals, and the same sort of comedy as me. He was different as well. With guys my age, it's so hard to get them to show interest. You have to work so hard, but he was up for a chat. He started discussions and stuff. So, that was nice.'

'And then, you met him in person?'

'Yeah. We met in person, about two weeks later. We went for a coffee, and I was so worried that I'd meet him and he wouldn't be the person I'd been talking to, which happens a lot. Or that … he would think that about me. But he was, like, exactly like I imagined. His appearance – but even the way he talked – was exactly how I imagined. The same phrases he used online. I really liked him.'

'And where did it go to from there?'

'We started hanging out and talking. We'd go out, and he'd stay at my place and I would stay at his, and we would chat online all day. We both kind of decided that we didn't want to be in a relationship or we didn't want to label it or anything. But we really got along – and things progressed pretty quickly.'

'So, you ended up in a relationship?'

'Well, here's the thing … I mean, we never really had that discussion, and I guess I thought we were seeing each other exclusively. Like, we spent a lot of time together. I remember for New Year's Eve, I stayed over at his house, and then his mum and I were making breakfast in the kitchen and stuff. I was kind of like part of his family … so, I guess I didn't feel like I had to have that conversation. And then a couple of months ago, it went a bit weird. We were seeing each other less, and then he stopped sending me so many messages. They were less frequent. I could tell something was up. So, I asked him, I said, you know, is something going on? And he said he was just super busy with work, and anxious and stuff. So, I left it – but it didn't get any better ... And then, a couple of weeks later, he said to me that he had been talking to another girl at the same time as me, and that he had figured out he liked her better, and wanted to, you know, formally, be in a relationship with her.

'I mean, what was I supposed to say? We had never had that conversation – and at the start we had sort of talked about seeing other people at the same time, so he'd not really done anything wrong. I guess I'd just never set up parameters around this, because I just assumed, you know?

'So, then he changed his profile on Facebook to "in a relationship". Straight after the conversation. So, I just blocked him and that was the end of that.'

'Did it upset you that it ended like that?'

'Yeah, absolutely. I was gutted. I spent weeks in bed,

crying. I mean, I felt like we had a real connection, and he was just seeing other people. It had a real hit on my confidence, my self-esteem. You know? I went off the apps for a period of time to get over it.'

'And now you're back?'

'Yeah, I'm back on. I sort of just went back on for sex, to be honest. I'm a fairly sexual person, so sometimes I just like to keep it to a flirtation, or even a hook-up.'

'And do you change your profile when you're looking for something more sexual?'

'Not really.'

'And how has that worked for you?'

'It's been mixed to be honest. Lately it's been a bit of a nightmare. I know a lot of the girls would say they don't want to send a nude or anything, but sometimes I enjoy a bit of sexting. But recently it's just been a bit … I don't know, gross.'

'What do you mean by that?'

'Well, you know, most guys you meet online ask you for a nude. Sometimes it's really early in the discussion ... out of the blue, they'll just want a nude, and it's out of context … and gross. And then they'll just send you their dick. Again, out of the blue. I'll be sitting on the bus and get a picture message on Snapchat or whatever, and it's a dick. It's so embarrassing. Then I have to block them. It's so disrespectful, but kind of like weird and accepted behaviour in the online space.'

'Do you ever take action around it?'

'Yeah, sometimes. Once I was chatting to a guy and he started sending me dick pics, and I figured out he was actually dating someone I knew – so I ended up taking a screen grab of the photo and pixellating it, and sharing it on my stories on Instagram to friends, and tagging his handle, so people knew he was a creep.'

'And are you online at the moment? Are you still trying to make a connection?'

'I mean, not now. I got tired of a lot of the behaviour, you know, so I went off. I think I just have to regroup a bit and go back to it. My self-esteem's been battered. I know my friends would say, you've got to get out there, but you know, I'm just fairly tired and a little bit disturbed by the whole thing. So, yeah, I need a break.'

4

The research and the social context

From a young age I was intrigued by the idea of love. As a child, I was introverted and strange. I buried myself in literature: the Bronte sisters, Shelley, Keats, Duras, and a good measure of Shakespeare. The type of white, Western education that nobody really wants much of these days. And alongside that, I imbibed a heavy dose of rom-coms. I was the last child and had two older sisters. There was a significant age gap between us, which meant I watched cult 1980s films with them at a very young age. Movies like

The Breakfast Club, Pretty in Pink, Sixteen Candles, and later, *Pretty Woman* and *Only You*.

It might have been this concoction of narrativised love which resulted in me being an overly romantic teenager. I was consumed by the idea of finding 'the one' and was quite sure that my life wouldn't start until that milestone had been achieved. In my 20s, and long before dating apps and online dating were conceptualised, I threw myself into the intimacy maelstrom with the type of passion only an idealist can summon. But as the years passed me by, and I accrued a collection of broken, damaged and unsuccessful relationships, I started to doubt the utopia of love. It occurred to me that the type of love that swept you away was reserved for the realm of literature and movies, or indeed, the imagination. Spaces which were highly fictionalised, orchestrated and, yes, imagined. Locations where the perfunctory and often awkward elements of real bodies didn't exist.

However, despite this pragmatic view on relationships, my fixation with the idea of love, romance and all things intimate continued. Never did it occur to me that love and intimacy might be a patriarchal tool. A way to maintain women's subservience. A measure to ensure continued labour in caring, keeping, bolstering, and even financing men.

In my late 30s, while working at one of those incredibly cool PR agencies with in-house table tennis tournaments, video games and an open bar, I found myself seated in an open-floor format where non-work conversations consistently revolved around the one topic – the interpretation of discussions, images and potential matches on dating apps. Having never used a dating app myself, these exchanges piqued my interest.

Many of my colleagues were in their early 20s and had not known a world sans dating apps – and although this didn't seem of particular relevance to them, I couldn't help but wonder, how did dating apps change intimacy? As intimacies (hook-ups, dates and romantic relationships) were filtered through the dating app architecture and infrastructure, what types of new intimacies were produced? Were gender stereotypes and scripts reinforced or subverted as a result of dating apps? And how did dating apps change or continue the milestones expected in romantic narratives?

The fieldwork conducted as part of my research occurred during March to June 2020, which coincided with the first COVID-19 lockdown in Australia – this also turned out to be unprecedented dating territory. With physical distancing orders in place, and most people either working or studying from home, dating apps became the key (if only) conduit for relationships. Dating apps across the world reported immense surges in sign-ups and use. This wasn't in and of itself revolutionary – with face-to-face meeting no longer possible, it was reasonable to imagine that the majority of singles or non-singles would turn towards dating apps to seek an intimate other. Alongside this, meeting an intimate other became increasingly important as singles faced the reality of lockdown alone. In a time of uncertainty, the desire for certainty, tradition, the known, became paramount.

I would contend that this digital revolution in the ambit of love and hook-ups was well underway prior to the COVID-19 lockdown. The pandemic perhaps accelerated the episodic use of dating apps, but they were already one of the main sources of relationship facilitation. Across the past two decades, dating apps have become a central point of discussion in relation to dating, relationships and intimacy.

Many Australian singles (and non-singles) frequently use an app or multiple apps to navigate and negotiate relationships.[1] Independent research indicates that rates of dating app usage have seen significant growth in Australia across the last decade.[2] A survey of 2000 people conducted by Nielsen in 2010 revealed that 25 per cent of Australians had tried dating apps. In 2015, Tinder announced that 15 per cent of the Australian population had joined the app. Most recently, a 2017 study conducted by YouGov indicated 52 per cent of Australian singles had used a dating app to make a romantic connection. The same study indicated, usage was particularly high for single Australians between 25 and 34, with 60 per cent having used a dating app to make a romantic connection.

Opinions relating to dating app usage in contemporary media have varied; however, an overarching narrative has emerged in which dating apps have colonised love, created a virtual emotional marketplace, fostered a hook-up culture and devalued traditional institutions such as marriage, monogamy and long-term partnerships. Other negative commentary has centred around health and concern over physical and emotional safety, as well as a perceived rise in sexually transmitted diseases (STDs) as a result of an app-facilitated hook-up culture.

For older generations who may never have used dating apps (or are suddenly required to foray into this space), censure of the dating app landscape is high; for younger generations (particularly those in the 18–28-year-old bracket), dating apps present as a pre-condition to romance, an integral part of the dating experience. This younger generation has never dated in an IRL (in real life) environment, and many would prefer not to.

In the 2020s, it is hard to imagine a world without dating apps or digitally facilitated relationships. In the past, computer-based match-making technology had its naissance in the 1960s, but its genealogy can be traced to personal ads in the 17th century. The first online dating site was kiss.com, which was registered in 1994, and the mid-90s saw a rise in similar matchmaking websites including match.com, RSVP.com and e-harmony.

The growth of relationship websites – and, subsequently, mobile dating apps – has been steady across the last 20 years. The last decade saw a panoply of dating apps mushroom, catering towards a diversity of groups and people. The shift to mobile dating app usage significantly changed the dynamic and made online dating ubiquitous. Users can now access matches from any location, and can also locate matches in situ (for example, by opening Tinder in a bar, users are able to see which singles are closest to them, based on the geospatial functionalities).

Leading the dating app charge was Grindr, a geosocial and networking dating app released in 2009, which is available on Android and iOS and can be downloaded from the app store. Tinder was released in 2011, and less than three years later (2014), the platform had registered over one billion users.[3] Since then, dating apps have flooded the market (Hinge, Scruff, Happn, Coffee meets Bagel, Bumble etc.), tailored to different segments of the community. But dating apps are now mainstream.

Today, the notion of love, relationships, hook-ups and dating are deeply entangled with dating apps. However, it is undoubtable that the digital world reconfigures 'everyday life' – particularly within the intimacy domain. Ling in his article, on the digital domain details this 'everydayness' in relation to texting and mobile phones, writing, 'Nobody sits at home anymore waiting for the phone to ring.'[4] And indeed, this Uber-planned approached to the digital and dating is continued within the app environment.

And although we would all like to condemn the digital domain as the genesis for the shallowness of the dating environment, there is little analysis of the deep continuities in love and intimacy which dating apps produce and facilitate. Dating apps present as a rupture in the way relationships are instigated and developed; that is, a movement from a physical environment to a digital landscape. However, they also present a *continuity* in pre-existing relationship dynamics and romantic masterplots. As my research demonstrates, despite the 'hook-up' dynamic generated by app architecture like Tinder, users continue to seek to emplot themselves in a romantic narrative.

As a snapshot of my work, I conducted iterative focus groups to gather shared understandings of dating apps but also to shake out any new and different ideas or ways of thinking around dating apps. The focus groups were conducted in Sydney city, and regional participants were provided the option of connecting via Zoom. Participants were asked set questions in the first focus group around their dating app experience, usage practices, personal presentation on apps, expectations, and desires. Questions were tailored for the second focus group around trends that emerged, and participants were also asked to design their ideal dating app architecture and functionalities in groups. In-depth interviews were conducted over Zoom and were approximately an hour in length, following a semi-structured format. Eight participants also journalled their experience during the month of March and were asked to do so for at least one hour per week, capturing screen grabs of their experience if they desired.

Twenty participants were recruited: twelve were heterosexual women, six were heterosexual men and two were queer men. Two participants were consensually non-monogamous, the rest were 'single' or were in the preliminary stages of dating ('talking to') someone. The research intended on capturing heterosexual dating app practices, although it did not seek to exclude other sexualities or ways of being.

Despite the hype around dating apps facilitating a hook-up culture, or rotational door of sexual partners, the majority of users tended to use dating apps to make romantic connections. This could have been a result of the uncertainty of COVID-19. They leant heavily on the romantic masterplot. A commonly known device and way to narrativise life in white, Western societies. In essence, we are indoctrinated to believe that key life milestones need to be met for us to have led a 'good life' or a 'worthy life' – and one of those is the romantic partnership.

These milestones have an order to them; for example, we study, find a job, become established, buy a property, fall in love, get married, procreate and so forth. If people mix things up – for example, have a child prior to getting married – they might say they 'did things out of order'. This confirms their understanding of a milestone system, equipped with temporal anxieties. Of course, such a system varies across cultures, and as indicated is specific to a white, Western way of thinking.

There is a clear heteronormativity in the romance masterplot and its milestones (for example, first date, moving in, marriage, conceiving a baby etc.), including its impetus towards the couple norm. The effect of this has been grappled with at length in queer theory. Professor of Anthropology, Tom Boellstorf talks about 'straight time' in his work, the way time is broken down in heterosexual relationships, or time well spent.

Questions of straight time were particularly interrogated during the debates over the legalisation of same-sex marriage, because – very broadly speaking – marriage is a clear marker in a narrative governed by straight time. As Boellstorff noted, there was significant tension between the desire of equal rights (i.e. the right to marry) and the desire to resist the imposition of a heteropatriarchal temporal narrative. There were not enough LGBTQ+ participants in the sample for me to make any substantive claims about how app users belonging to these communities interact with the romance masterplot and how any resistance to 'straight time' might complicate this.

However, a predominant heterosexual narrative was consistently evoked. For many this was done so with ire; sometimes it even had a depressive quality to it. It was almost as though the individuals involved were disappointed that this was the only way a heterosexual love story could unfold, but were equally unable to come up with different forms of expression.

My research focussed on heterosexual intimacies, particularly because I was interested in the way dating apps, the romantic masterplot and ways of representing oneself impacted the power balance between men and women in romantic relationships. However, I sought not to exclude queer participants, and as I describe later in the book (see Chapter twelve), they often shone a light on critical issues within the dating app paradigm and in relationship dynamics.

Notably, questions of gender are fundamental to dating apps. They are foundational to app algorithms, as this is the key way in which a user indicates their preference as to whose profiles the app will show them. There have been several studies examining apps through the lens of gender. Academic researchers Caitlin Macleod and Victoria McArthur argue, in their analysis of the respective interfaces of Tinder and Bumble, that 'gender is constructed within the apps both implicitly and explicitly'. They note that though gender is 'intrinsic to the technical aspects of the apps, Bumble and Tinder structure it in a way that is useful to their design rather than accommodating of nuanced and varied lived experiences of gender'.

Stefanie Duguay, an Assistant Professor in the Department of Communication Studies at Concordia University in Montreal, Canada, notes that because Tinder relies on Facebook as a kind of guarantor that users on the app are authentic, it benefits from Facebook fostering presentable users who abide by norms, and it draws a direct line between authenticity and normativity in its marketing materials by emphasising young white heterosexual people.

Sociology researcher Kenneth Hanson has also found that app use among heterosexual college students reinforces whiteness and gendered norms.

Even on apps which target LGBTQ+ users, such as Grindr, an app predominantly for gay men, heteronormativity is evident, with users often rejecting potential partners who do not fit a normative ideal, in that they might be 'older, black, short, fat, with long hair, and, mainly … effeminate'.

Similarly, a study of bisexual women using Tinder in New Zealand found that these users were positioned 'as "outsiders" in a heteronormative and biphobic domain'.

The gendered scripts and attitudes expressed in, via and around dating apps are necessarily inflected with place. This is another foundational aspect to dating app algorithms – they are location-aware, as they seek to match users with prospective partners in the same geographical radius. There can be distinct differences in the ways people use dating apps at home versus when they are travelling. For example, when staying in an unfamiliar city, users might feel a lot freer in their app use than in a small town where they live, where they run a much higher risk of encountering people they know on the app.

The sexual scripts mobilised by users was of particular interest to me. By sexual scripting I mean the ways in which participants felt they had to behave or should behave in order to attract a match. These sexual scripts emerged both in how users presented themselves on apps and how they interacted with the apps. Several gendered and culturally specific notions emerged during my research, including the ideas of the 'high maintenance woman' and the 'Aussie bloke'.

The 'Aussie bloke' is a modern incarnation of the bushman, the ANZAC, the surfer boy. He is muscular, sporty, attractive, humorous, relaxed and, yes, white. This was intensely 'othering' (caused feelings of exclusion and marginalisation) for men in the sample who were culturally diverse or Indigenous, but curiously, it was also othering for white men, who felt they could never live up to the cultural ideals exemplified by the 'Aussie bloke'.

In essence, the majority of men felt they were doing masculinity wrong, and their dating app experience left them feeling marginalised and 'shit about themselves'. However, dating apps are not the only way we communicate or develop intimacies and are not the best way to facilitate an intimacy. Online dating is an intensely 'white' space, and masculinity online is often seen through a white lens.

Different cultural groups interact in different ways from an intimacy perspective – many without the assistance of a dating app or white-world dating apps like Tinder or Bumble. It's important to note this: there is a whole world of intimacy that doesn't include dating apps.

I include a chapter on sexual racism, othering and representation of masculinity, although it deserves a whole separate analysis (and potentially book). For this book, I focus on the 'high maintenance woman': how she is described, how she is packaged, and what this means more broadly for women and heterosexual relationships.

We don't come to our dating app use, or even our negotiations of love, as though from a void. We have pre-existing ideas on the topics which act as a fulcrum for how we interact with the apps, and indeed other people. I sought to contextualise the pre-existing knowledge users had as they entered the dating app and intimacy domain in 2020. While I was conducting this research, a media dialogue was swirling around the safety of dating apps, and at the same time, the media was reporting about their fervent usage. This included print media, blogs, television and radio.

I used one case study in particular to describe the flavour of media reporting at the time, a *Four Corners* story which garnered widespread media attention in 2020. There were several large holes in the reporting of this story, which seemed to invite the condemnation of dating apps as the source of growing sexual assault numbers in Australia. In particular, the story should be focused on the safety (or lack thereof) of women on dating apps – quietly and ever so stealthily removing sexual agency from many women. Much reporting about dating apps contains misinformation, and it's unclear whether or not this is because the reporting is intentionally sensationalised as clickbait or if the journalists involved have never used dating apps (and hence report distortions). A dating app is a cloistered world: unlike Facebook or Instagram, you simply can't google a dating app and have an insider's look; without an account, you'll never fully experience the dating app maelstrom.

I also focused on the media messaging which proliferated during COVID-19 about the massive jump in dating app usage worldwide. The media (including myself) reported immense surges in downloads and usage, including swiping and direct messages. We all hypothesised about the rationale for this spike, but it was difficult to isolate the cause: was it a fear of loneliness (for those told to socially isolate alone)? Was it the COVID-19 time compression accordion – which made people feel frozen in time, desperate to reach life milestones or at least have a sense that they were moving forward? Was it pragmatic? Likely, it was a combination of these things and then some.

Case study 1: Patriarchal reporting

In October 2020, *Four Corners* aired a program which investigated Tinder titled 'Tinder and how digital dating became a predators' playground'.[5] The investigation was a collaboration with Triple J's current affairs radio program *Hack* and purported to 'reveal that the dating app was a playground for sexual offenders'. In advance of the report, *Four Corners* and *Hack* put a call out to find people who had 'safety concerns' around dating apps. Four hundred people responded. Two hundred and thirty-one of these people had used Tinder and of these, forty-eight people indicated they had experienced sexual violence from a person they had met on Tinder – this might include abusive messages, images or physical violence.

The program, which aired on 10 October 2020, created widespread community condemnation of Tinder. News outlets like news.com and Mamamia followed suit with stories around the 'dark side of Tinder'.[6] Junkee ran a story with the headline 'Absolutely Sickening'.[7] Buried deep within the report was the core element – that 48 people had reported sexually abusive behaviours on Tinder, but only 11 of those people had received a response. The kernel of the story related to the way Tinder dealt with sexual abuse reports and the organisation's willingness to collaborate with authorities within the justice space.

However, this story was enveloped by a broader narrative: Tinder is not a safe place for women.

The article and program featured all-female case studies – in particular, two women who were raped by men they had met on Tinder. The faces of women who had provided their testimonies were used to illustrate the article (some blurred out). The associated ABC digital news article drew out the specifics relating to one case. The woman described how she had matched with the rapist on Tinder and had agreed to meet with him, not knowing his surname, mobile number or any other personal details. The media release issues by *Four Corners/Hack* led with a quote from a father:

'It's like a minefield ... It's a perfect platform for predators and scammers.'

It was unclear whether this 'father' had used Tinder, or where this information was gleaned from. However, *Four Corners/Hack* positioned this quote as the lead statement, above the testimony of women who had been raped.

In publishing this story, *Four Corners* and *Hack* sought to expose the predatory nature of Tinder and, to some extent, empower women by telling the women's stories. But there was nothing empowering in the storytelling. Recounting a story of a woman who had been raped by a man she had met on Tinder, and not secured any of his personal details, *invited the flagrant questioning of her character.* Positioning a father's voice as the key statement indicated to the reader that a man's voice (even one that had never used the dating app before) was the most important and legitimate source. The act of not describing how dating logistics are navigated in the online domain seemed an attempt to only narrate parts of the story – and those parts which built an argument in relation to women being unsafe on Tinder.

The report didn't include statistics to describe the nature of sexual assault in Australia (a broader discussion – not simply reducible to just Tinder). Another omission was the singular focus on women without attention paid to other vulnerable groups (like non-binary members of the community), or reference to points of intersectionality (for example, Indigenous, culturally and linguistically diverse (CALD), queer or even remote or regional Australians). This package highlighted how contemporary media focus conflates intimacy and sex with danger and violence specifically within the dating app space.

In 2021, Australia experienced its own #metoo movement

after Brittany Higgins, former Liberal Party staffer, came forward, describing how she had been raped by the acting chief of staff of the then Defence Minister's Office, Linda Reynolds, in Parliament House in the lead up to the 2018 election.[8] Higgins reported the rape at the time, only to be silenced by critical figures within the political system. Following Higgins' testimony, a series of other women came forward with similar reports.[9]

The Australian political system was rocked and a light was shone on the violent misogyny which was occurring at the highest echelons. Women across Australia came forward with their stories, which culminated in the Justice Marches which happened across Australian capital cities.[10] In light of these occurrences, and this reckoning, it's hard to imagine the *Four Corners* and *Hack* story running in 2021 – as it has now become abundantly clear that Tinder is not the genesis or only perpetrating force of sexual assault in Australia – and that sexual assault can allegedly occur within places where we would expect the highest levels of integrity (like federal Parliament House). In addition, it is not limited to interactions with strangers as implied in the *Four Corners* and *Hack* story – via the woman who had not collected the details of her rapist in advance of meeting him.

The story indicated that message threads could be deleted on Tinder, making it difficult to surface evidence relating to rape or sexual abuse. This is a common feature on many messaging and social media platforms, including Instagram, WhatsApp and iPhone messaging. The news program did not indicate that most people progress the 'date logistics' on a separate platform to Tinder; for example, on WhatsApp or Instagram (which, as indicated, have similar deletion features), or that in relation to the sending and receipt of explicit images, Tinder has no image send functionality (hence explicit images are sent or received on other platforms). Instead, the program and associated articles positioned Tinder as the genesis or exacerbator of sexual abuse – the 'predators' playground'.

Why was Tinder in particular, despite a suite of other dating apps, the priority focus for this story? In addition, why was Tinder positioned as the genesis of sexual assault or a 'predators' playground'? And why were women depicted as vulnerable (incapable of gathering vital details to ensure their own sexual protection) within the reporting? Finally, why was the legitimate source a 'father'? It all seemed to flagrantly point to the need for women to become invisible. It demanded that women dispose of their sexual agency and hand the reins over to their father.

Here, any woman who was visible in the online dating app space was asking for it.

Case study 2: COVID-19

My research was collected during the first half of 2020 – which coincided with the start of the COVID-19 pandemic and lockdown in NSW. This meant that participants were in a unique dating paradigm – the digital domain represented the only space in which singles could mingle. Of course, this wasn't just dating apps – participants within my research indicated they were sliding into people's DMs via Instagram, Snapchat, TikTok or even LinkedIn.

However, in March 2020 (the start of lockdown in NSW) the hyper-usage of dating apps became a key topic in the media.

The discussion commenced in the media and subsequently exploded across popular culture on 3 March 2020, when Tinder issued an in-app public service announcement (PSA) regarding COVID-19. This was greeted with a panoply of memes and gags across social and mainstream media. [11]

The Tinder PSA read:

Your WellBeing Is Our #1 Priority

Tinder is a great place to meet new people. While we want you to continue to have fun, protecting yourself from the Coronavirus is more important. Here are some of the tips to keep in mind:

Wash your hands frequently

Carry hand sanitizer

Avoid touching your face

Maintain social distance in public gatherings.

Tinder then provided its users with a link directing them to the World Health Organization (WHO) website. Bumble's company spokespeople spoke directly with online newspaper *TMZ*, revealing that their global customer service team was directing their users to the CDC and WHO sites for up-to-date info on the current coronavirus pandemic.

Suddenly, dating apps were front and centre in the media and within the social media barrage. Twitter became a haven for comments such as, 'When Tinder turns into your household doctor, you know you're in trouble.'

This intense media focus coincided with an uplift in app usage numbers as a significant shift in usage and behaviour:

This shift has increased the number of dating app users

> *and the amount of time people spend on dating apps. Tinder says its users had 11 per cent more swipes and 42 per cent more matches last year, making 2020 the apps busiest year.*[12]

Between 5 and 10 March, OkCupid reported a 7 per cent increase in new conversations,[13] and at the same time, ten out of the top 100 apps on the iTunes Store were dating apps.[14] During the second week of March, active users on Bumble rose by 8 per cent.[15] As American cities went into lockdown, apps reported increased numbers of messaging. On Bumble from 12–22 March, Seattle saw a 23 per cent increase in sent messages, New York City, 23 per cent and San Francisco, 26 per cent.[16] This was a trend that was reported worldwide – with the then CEO of Tinder, Elie Seidman, indicating the rise of an episodic use of dating apps, which coincided with cities going into lockdown.[17]

Dating apps, however, are intended to facilitate a face-to-face meeting, which was no longer possible within the COVID-19 lockdown landscape. Dating apps sought to facilitate this shift in interactions by catering to a largely digital paradigm. For example, Tinder and Bumble introduced video chat capabilities.

Social media also pointed to another interesting trend:

DM chats were becoming largely Covid-centric. In the month of March, OkCupid reported a 188 per cent increase in the number of profiles which mentioned COVID-19.[18] Indian Tinder users also described a rise in longer DM chats, and media started to report this as a return to a Jane-Austen-like style of courtships. COVID-19 threatened to flatten the casual hook-up and instead reinstate the old school romance of a Jane-Austen-esque world. Instead of love letters, video and DM chats were the new forms of dialogue within these dating app courtships.

I weighed into the media debate, with my own articles in *The Conversation*, *The New Daily* and even spots on daytime television. Here's what I had to say:

> *In this new world, we're all navigating how romantic intimacy can exist without physical contact.*
>
> *With the prospect of months of self-isolation how will we navigate sex? After all, not everyone has a sexual partner readily available.*
>
> *A notice about sex and coronavirus from the New York City Department of Health went viral last weekend. It included the statement 'You are your safest sex partner'.*
>
> *The tables are suddenly turned: online hook-ups were*

previously framed as less wholesome than face-to-face ones. Yet in 2020 they are perceived as safer.

Connection is sought after in times of uncertainty, risk and crisis. But COVID-19 makes the navigation of these intimacies certainly difficult. We are in the middle of a historical re-jigging of our understanding of romance, intimacy and sex.

It's safe to say the negotiation of intimacy has been irrevocably changed – even if it is only for the short while.[19]

It was an incredibly topical issue – but did the media drive this usage fervour by reporting about the surge in numbers and hypothesising as to why? And did the media similarly drive a sense of FOMO (fear of missing out) and a need to participate in the lovemaking scene for the Covid-lockdown period (timeframe unknown)? However, it's safe to say there were two key main media angles on dating apps during Covid lockdown:

1. Patriarchal reporting (moral panic about dating apps and their impact on love, romance and dating, as well as safety implications);
2. Immense surges in usage (FOMO, get in there or lose out).

Importantly, this is the lens through which participants (users) approached my research.

And in this environment, the high maintenance woman emerged.

5

Kristina: The 'tomboy' and the 'Aussie bloke'

Kristina is a 30-year-old nurse who lives in Penrith. When we chat, we're in the thick of the Sydney lockdown and the initial euphoria of our lockdown lives has worn off, especially for those working in health care, who are still considered essential workers. Kristina lives with a housemate.

'So, tell me a bit about yourself, Kristina.'

'Well, I'm a bit of a self-confessed tomboy. I don't know if that's an outdated term … I'm assuming it is. I'm not really the cool type or anything.'

We're conducting this interview via Zoom and Kristina is sitting on her bed, beaming in via her laptop. A commonplace set-up in most of my interviews. She's wearing a loose black T-shirt and a beanie.

'What do you mean by tomboy?'

'Well, you know, I'm not a girly girl. My standard get-up is jeans and some Connies. I don't do makeup, and I have a motorbike. I grew up with boys on a rural farm, so I'm a bit boyish. But, I'm not a lesbian; everyone always thinks because you're a bit of a tomboy, you're a lesbian, but I'm very heterosexual.' She shakes her head as though this distinction is difficult for people to make.

'Have you found yourself explaining that a lot?'

'Yeah, a lot. People just don't get it. I'm just a bit blokey almost. But I'm not gay. It's been really tough from an identity perspective. I feel like I've constantly got this tension between being myself and then pretending to be more like a girl. It's been like that since I was a kid.'

'Tell me a bit about what dating apps you're using and why you're using them.'

'Well, to begin with – I think it's a bit of a joke, but then on the other side of things, I also understand they're one of the only ways you can meet someone these days. So, you know, up until my mid-20s, I had no issues meeting men, even if I was a tomboy. I guess I was lucky that way. I always met them face-to-face, at school, at work, whatever…. And I would say they were long-term relationships. But some of them were a bit toxic. After my mid-20s, I kind of felt like I had to work on myself first, and then get to the relationship side of things – and I did that. And then in my late 20s, I was like, hang on ... I'm just not meeting anyone face-to-face anymore. In a short period of time, everyone went online and I just had to adapt.'

'And what apps are you using now?'

'Mostly Hinge. I went on Bumble initially, but no-one was matching or responding, it was absolutely dead, so I went to Hinge. Tinder's just not my vibe, you know?'

'Do you think it's a bit more of a hook-up app?'

'Yeah, it's like the bro-app. I'm not really into that – I'm looking for a relationship.'

'And why do you think Bumble wasn't working for you?'

'I don't know … I mean, I think men find it weird when you start the chat. Even if that's how the app is constructed. It's a patriarchal thing where they feel affronted by women suddenly starting the chat, so they just don't respond. It's weird I guess. Also, it was before I changed my profile.'

'You changed your profile?'

'Yeah, when I started on dating apps, I was like, authentic. I put up some pics of me, me and my motorbike, me in Bali, me bungy-jumping – I'm an adventurous, free spirit type, and I like motorbikes, but it was literally crickets. So, then I showed my mum my profile, and my mum and I have this odd bond. We're super close. She's a psychologist – and she's always giving me advice about this sort of stuff. She thinks I'm on the shelf and will end up a spinster … she said, you need to be more feminine in your profile, put up some pics of you in dresses – still looking natural, of course, but the more feminine side of things. I didn't want to initially, because I never look like that, but eventually, I buckled. I change my profile to these cute images of me, and reduced my bio to like a couple of words like nurse, star sign, and that's about it … boom, I'm getting all these hits, all these DMs … the world suddenly changes.'

'And do you find that off-putting?'

'Yes, of course! Because it's not me! And I think, do I really want to go on a date with someone who wants this type of girl?'

'What type of girl do you mean?'

'Oh, you know this pretty, nicey-nicey type. Makes me

want to vomit in my mouth. And then disturbingly … I find myself acting like that girl, in the chats, like I have half a brain, and they love it! It's actually a real mind-fuck.'

'So, do you go on any dates with these people?'

'No. That's the thing. I can't be bothered – because I know it's fake, fake, fake. But in the background my mum's there telling me that my biological clock is ticking, and I need to secure a man ASAP or forever hold my peace, and I won't lie to you, it stresses me out. Especially because of Covid. Now, in lockdown, I think, is this all there is? Will I ever meet anyone?'

'What makes you feel like that?'

'It's like everything has ground to a halt, and it's just the minutiae of everyday life, that's it. And I think will I ever get my own life … will it ever start?'

'Have you felt lonely across this period?'

'Yeah, I guess. Even though I still go to work – and I have a housemate, who is my best friend. But she's met someone and they're always together, and it makes me feel like, am I ever going to have that? And then there's my mum in the background telling me the clock's ticking, and this ridiculous fake situation on the apps.'

'Have you ever thought about reversing your profile,

going back to the original one?'

'No, I mean, it's proven … it just doesn't work. I have been going on TikTok … it's really taken off during Covid, but I find there's a lot of guys there, the kind of guys I'm interested in, and it's less of a contrived environment. I might follow someone's reel and then drop them a message at some point. It's not that weird fake vibe and there's less focus on what I look like, because you can see more of my personality, if that makes sense.'

'Yeah, I see what you mean. And what type of guys are you interested in?'

'Well, I guess I like Aussie blokes.'

'What do you mean by that?'

'Well, you know, because I'm kind of tall and a tomboy, I like a bigger man, you know with hair on his chest, a beard. Aussie humour, a bit of a larrikin. Someone that can go out and camp … I'm a camping type, not a hotel type of a girl, you know what I mean?'

'Yeah, I guess I've not heard that term in a long time. So, overall, what do you make of dating apps?'

'Look, I'm going to be honest, I get that their functionality is all around matching people, and hooking people up, but I think they do the opposite – it's almost like they split people apart. If you think about me, I've now got this fake dating app profile. I'm pretending to be someone, but to what end? I don't actually go on any dates from it. So, I'm kind of just wasting time. And it's reinforcing this awful stereotype in my mind that men only want certain types of women – basic, pretty, nice women. Not challenging women. Not smart women. Not free spirits, and definitely not tomboys. It's like I'm being forced into this shape, and I'm resisting all the way – but it's the only one that will get me the outcomes. What's on the other side of that? Being alone – and to be honest, I'm not okay with that.'

6

The high maintenance woman: Who is she?

In my early 20s, I went to a house party in Canberra with my new boyfriend. He wasn't the typical guy that I dated. I'm culturally diverse, my parents are Italian migrants, I'm first generation Australian, and I tended to socialise with other migrant kids. We shared similar characteristics. We were culturally diverse. Our parents were different. They tended to be stricter, and even had a separate set of values. We were also similar in that we had previously been '*othered*': we understood what it was like to be on the fringes.

I had dated 'Aussie' guys before, but I had never really *dated them*. As in, they weren't the type of people I would ever bring home to meet my strict Italian parents. They were flirtations, short romances, dalliances, casual sex. On this occasion, and separated from my parents who lived in Sydney, I'd managed to develop a longer-term relationship with this 'Aussie' guy.

That house party was the first time I was meeting his friends, and I was suitably nervous.

I was, and am, the type of person who takes pride in their appearance. Fashion was an art form for me. I loved bright colours, form-fitting dresses, different textures, and heels. I've always had a passion for handbags.

That evening, I'd put on a form-fitting dress, with long earrings and a pair of outrageous heels. When I arrived at the event I discovered that I was not just overdressed, I was *ridiculously* overdressed. It was a thongs and jeans kind of an affair.

Interestingly, there was also a curious gender divide happening; the women were perched on one side of the party and the men on the other.

Never one to be deterred, I enthusiastically said hello, and ended up staying on the men's side of the discussion. After a couple of ill-fated attempts at engagement with the blokes I discovered that my colourful social commentary was not quite their speed. In fact, my questions were met with one-word responses, and then silence.

Finally, I retreated to the women's discussion – which was more expansive, and less obtuse.

As the evening progressed and the drinks continued, the group became rowdier, looser with their conversation. At a certain point in the evening, I found myself in earshot of my new guy and a friend of his, and started to understand that the discussion they were having was about me. The other guy said, 'I mean she's good-looking and everything, but don't you want someone a bit more, you know, down to earth?'

Had I not presented a down-to-earth, engaging persona? There had been nothing pretentious about my actions that evening, nor do I consider myself to be pretentious generally. Colourful, yes, but never stuck-up. My new boyfriend didn't spring to my defence following this criticism.

'Don't you want someone relatable? Like, she seems like hard work.'

Again, no response from my man.

'She uses these long words … like, fuck, are you serious?'

At that point a third party entered the conversation, and they steered towards another topic. I was fuming. My cheeks coloured and my heart pounded. I found myself instantly unable to engage with the discussion that was occurring with the group of women around me.

But I contained myself. I knew an emotional reaction would confirm exactly what my boyfriend's friend had said about me – that I was high maintenance. And although those exact words had not been mentioned in the dialogue, they were inherently implied.

I was the difficult girlfriend. The one who wanted things. Who had an opinion. Who was expensive. Who was *foreign.*

At that point in time, I didn't even bother unpicking those concepts and why they were linked together.

The thing is, I had grown up knowing I was in the 'difficult' category, and I had worked hard to make myself 'relatable'. What made me difficult? Well, I was dux of my year, every single high school year running, I had an outstanding academic transcript and in my early 20s I had a double degree and master's. I also had disorderly eating, and a fixation with maintaining a certain weight. Finally, I was a feminist, and I didn't mind saying it. I wasn't just going to sit with the women's circle at the party, I was definitely going to break the gender divide.

I had learnt over the years that this made me a *difficult partner*. I never went with the flow, and I always had to say something. Of course, I had no intention of changing.

But I had developed coping mechanisms – like being overly friendly and being humorous. I discovered over the years that sometimes those things aren't enough; when you're deemed high maintenance, there is no turning back.

Just under 20 years came and went, and over those years, I met people who were equally academic, quirky, eccentric, and who loved me. I moved to the inner city of Sydney, and soon I was surrounded by a clique of like-minded extravagants.

It wasn't lost on me that I could only date a certain type of man. As one ex pointed out to me as we were breaking up – it was difficult to date a radical. I'm not sure what made me a radical, but I'd been labelled.

I was high maintenance. However, I didn't connect this with a broader category and to patriarchy, until much later, through my research.

Men in my sample sought to portray themselves as the 'Aussie bloke'; women portrayed themselves *against* the idea of 'high maintenance'.

The term 'high maintenance' is part of the common vernacular, and usually refers to a woman. In my interviews the term most prevalently (and patronisingly) used was 'high maintenance *girl*'.

In the romantic hit *When Harry Met Sally*, Harry uses the term to describe Sally and her very specific way of ordering food. She responds, 'I just want it the way I want it.' After they have been friends awhile, Sally has a personal crisis and calls Harry in distress. She describes herself as 'too difficult' and to comfort her he replies that she is merely 'challenging'. Eventually, yes, we all know it, they fall in love. However, Sally confirms the cultural narrative that a woman who 'wants it the way she wants it' is high maintenance or at best 'challenging'.

The 'high maintenance girl' I found in my research was slippery and hard to define. A mixture of behavioural and physical traits were used to describe 'high maintenance'. An often-regurgitated characteristic was being too 'done-up'. As one participant (Rose) indicated:

> *Tinder was all photos, so I would just pick photos I thought I looked the best in. And then I had a friend go through it [my profile], and they said, 'You just don't come across as the person that you are; like, you've got*

> *all these glamour photos, and all when you're dressed up nicely, and it gives off the wrong impression of you. People feel like you're very high maintenance...' And I looked back at it and I thought, you don't want to come across like that. So, then I put in lower key photos, when I'm not dressed up, full makeup and about to go out on the town.*

Women sought to create a 'pretty but relatable' view of themselves, one that established that they were 'lower key' and amenable. However, critically, they also had to portray themselves as classically feminine. Kristina (described in Chapter 5) has struggled with identity management since childhood and believed herself to be too much of a tomboy. She felt she needed to dial down the elements of her profile that were perceived as too masculine:

> *Well, I'm definitely not a girly girl. I'm more of a tomboy. So, I've tried to not make it just bikes and stuff. I've tried to make it more girly. I've struggled a bit with that, though, because I think a lot of men can be a bit intimidated by that. My mum, if you can believe it, told me I needed to put more feminine photos in my photo. So, I ended up using this image of me at a wedding with a dress on and lipstick ... suddenly I was getting all these matches ... makes me feel weird, though ... I never look like that.*

Women had a strong sense that they had to portray a certain cultural ideal to 'snag' a man online, which seemed to confirm known cultural narratives around women having to secure a man. Being too good-looking or sexy might lead to being perceived as high maintenance. They sought to curtail certain elements of their personas or elevate others to create the required picture.

Attractiveness came with a price tag, which I will explore later in Chapter 10. Curiously, beauty features like a heaving cleavage, pouty, hyper-filled lips and extensions were described with disgust. Women with this kind of 'porn' beauty, and who had undergone cosmetic surgery, were viewed with distaste. They were perceived either through a 'slut' or 'high maintenance' lens.

In contrast, these appearance ideals continue to be the ones women are told to aspire to through contemporary culture, with the majority of women represented in the limelight having this 'porn star look'.

Feminists have argued against the hyper-sexualisation of women for decades, and in particular how the appearance of women represented in porn has come to insidiously drift into the everyday woman's appearance.

In the West, cosmetic surgery is increasingly normalised.

Ninety per cent of plastic surgeries in Australia are performed on women. Almost 50,000 Australian women underwent a breast augmentation last year in Australia, and the number of labiaplasties has almost tripled in five years world-wide. The emotional cost of conforming to hyper-sexualisation is enormous for girls and young women who are in the process of forming their gender and sexual identity. We construct our identities through complex processes of interaction with the culture around us. An American Psychological Association study on girls' sexualisation found that it 'has negative effects in a variety of domains, including cognitive functioning, physical and mental health, sexuality, and attitudes and beliefs'. Some of these effects include risky sexual behaviour, higher rates of eating disorders, depression and low self-esteem, and reduced academic performance. Of course, there are girls who resist, but there are real social penalties to be paid by those who do not conform to acceptable feminine appearance.

In their online profiles, women are required to be sexualised, and yet rejected when they are too 'high maintenance'. This is the tightrope I discussed in my introduction. It's an impossible balance that no woman is capable of striking.

In my research, high maintenance women were described as having expensive taste, from the handbags they carried to the clothes they wore, to the places they went to (as identified in their images). These were all cultural prompts that male participants noticed and chalked up as being high maintenance. Again, women were placed in a lose-lose situation. Told by contemporary culture and the marketing industry to buy the right handbag as a symbol of success, and at the same time, berated for acquiring the object.

Behavioural characteristics of high maintenance women were also evoked. For example, pretentious bio descriptions that articulated jobs, academic success or even simply hinted to an expensive lifestyle. One participant who had her bio set as '*Living a Champagne lifestyle on a beer budget*' was told by friends that her bio description came across as too high maintenance (I talk about this more in Chapter 10).

Similarly, trying to move men along on the face-to-face meet-up journey, or even suggesting the first date, was seen as too forward. Men were expected to make the first move, and this was indicated by both men and women. For many women, this was hidden behind statements like:

I'm a bit traditional, I like guys to make the first move.

And:

We end up doing everything for them anyway; surely, at the beginning they can do something for us?

This statement demonstrates the labour involved in a heterosexual relationship – particularly when it comes to looking after housework, caring and planning.

High maintenance also related to intellectual or success markers. Aero-spatial female engineers for example, received the left swipe; teaching students did not.

The romantic masterplot for women

Many of the women in the sample (which was 18–35-year-olds), had a strong sense that the 'clock was ticking'. This was particularly relevant when it came to women 27 and over. It wasn't necessarily a biological, children ticking clock, it was more about the sense that they should have met a series of certain milestones, and they hadn't done so yet. Critical to these relationship milestones was meeting a life partner (the romantic masterplot). Again, for many, there was a sense that if they hadn't encountered a romantic partner their lives had not fully started. Almost as though the romantic milestone would trigger the beginning of adult life itself.

This was often diluted with a follow-up sense of ambivalence. However, it was a throwaway line, seemingly a rehearsed sentiment, something that they felt they should say rather than believed. One participant indicated:

> *I always get this sense – that my life hasn't quite started … like, if I got the right job, or had the right relationship … then it will all begin. My brothers and sisters are all married, and are having kids … they all met people face-to-face. Instead, I have to meet someone online! And I'm still single! But then sometimes I think … fuck that … who cares if I don't meet someone?*

Here there was also the indication that meeting someone in a digital environment was not the right way to emplot oneself in a romantic masterplot. There was an understood chain of events that should occur when you meet a lasting partner, and they were face-to-face. The majority of participants, including men, thought that a significant relationship should have a 'story', and that wasn't a story which involved a digital beginning. The meet cute was a significant part of these meetings.

The 'meet cute' is the moment in which two unlikely

people encounter each other while going about their ordinary lives, and something extraordinary begins. You may have seen this described beautifully by the delightful Arthur to Iris in the romantic comedy *The Holiday*.

The meet cute is a magical moment of happenstance. The people involved aren't looking for love (at least, not right then).

In 1991, Roger Ebert rather prosaically described the meet cute as 'a comic situation contrived entirely for the purpose of bringing a man and a woman together, after which they can work out their destinies for the remainder of the film'.

However you describe it, the meet cute is unexpected. It happens when romance is the furthest thing from the characters' minds. But in real life, in the age of online dating, more Australians meet their partner online than through friends and work.

Is it possible to have a meet cute on a dating app?

On dating apps, those looking for a relationship are searching for compatibility and chemistry, not conflict — for someone they could build a connection with, not the most unlikely person possible.

Many women felt they weren't attractive or special

enough for the meet cute to happen to them. That the meet cute was reserved for a super-human kind of woman. One participant indicated:

> *I'd like to meet someone in person. But where am I going to meet them? On the bus? I'm no Jennifer Lopez; nobody is just going to start talking to me on the bus. Besides, I'm kind of awkward. I would barely respond.*

Curiously, Jennifer Lopez was often referenced in relation to the meet cute.

Hence women felt relegated to the digital environment. Despondent about being there, and yet needing to be there to trigger the relationship milestone. And all the while aiming to be pretty but relatable.

The hook-up versus romance

The majority of women within the sample were seeking a committed monogamous relationship via dating apps. Despite the media buzz relating to Tinder being a 'hook-up' app and Bumble being a 'relationship' app, participants thought they were essentially very similar, and for the most part, the same people had profiles on both apps.

However, women seeking hook-ups and relationships at times had two separate profiles, or used two different apps.

One participant indicated that she used Tinder for hook-ups, and had crafted a highly sexualised profile (a series of images of her body, and the bio 'Here for a good time not a long time'), and used Hinge for dating and relationships (with a different, more relationship-oriented profile). She said: '*I've always been really sexual, and I enjoy a hook-up. But I keep my eye on the prize.*'

By the 'prize' she was referring to the committed, romantic relationship. Echoed throughout the research was the notion that the monogamous-companionate relationship was the 'prize' or the 'gold standard'.

The hook-up for most women was a required activity to satisfy sexual needs. Many of these women had used apps to hook up, and had positive experiences from these intimacies.

One woman within the sample used Tinder to hook up with over 30 men across 30 days to get her sexual independence back, after being ghosted by someone she felt intimately connected with. She organised the logistics around the hook-ups, and was specific about the time, location and sexual activity. She indicated: '*I say when. I say how.*'

As these were 'only' hook-ups she would often make

men travel to her home. When asked if she'd ever felt physically at risk, she said no. All of the men had stuck to the agreement and been respectful. This seemed to fly in the face of media commentary that dating apps caused or enticed sexual assault, or that women should fear dating apps/sexual encounters negotiated over dating apps.

This participant indicated she felt empowered as a result of her hook-up dating app use.

French feminist and academic Luce Irigaray argues that a key element to the patriarchy is the 'legitimate exchange of women' – from father to husband, categorised by walking down the aisle, and then evidenced by the changing of the surname. Irigaray argues that this means women, their futures and sexual partners are negotiated between men. They are but chattel in this shifting of pawns on an intimate chessboard. Dating apps disrupt this process – instead placing women in a position of power, able to choose their sexual partner. Hence the potential patriarchal media noise around women, safety and dating apps. Hence the positioning of the 'father' as a legitimate testimony in the *Four Corners* story.

Insidiously, women's sexual freedoms were being curbed.

Both women and men within the focus groups and

interviews held firmly to the idea that a hook-up couldn't be developed into a relationship, which demonstrated an ingrained understanding of how romantic milestones should occur – that is, sex had to occur at a certain point within a romantic relationship, and it wasn't the first step. It seemed to indicate that a romantic link had to exist first prior to a sexual interaction.

For women, there was a step change in behaviour. In relation to hook-ups, they could be demanding, factual, upfront – they said when and how, but when it came to a romantic liaison and relationship they needed to take the backseat, allowing men to take the driver's seat.

The cool, chill girl didn't demand anything from relationships (see Amelia's interview in Chapter 3). They were looking for a 'connection' and they sought to not put 'heavy parameters' around a fledgling relationship.

7

Rose: Living a Champagne life on a beer budget

Rose is 30, she lives in Clovelly in a share house. She has two flatmates, both single women of a similar age. She has a degree in Communications and a master's in public policy, and she grew up in Canberra. In her mid-20s she left Canberra and headed to the promised land, the bright lights, the glitz and glamour of Sydney. She began working at an advertising agency, and she quickly became a local in a world of frenetic busyness, where the importance of someone is judged by how many events they currently have in their social diary. Make yourself too available, and it becomes quickly obvious that you're a nobody.

'Canberra was a nice place … quiet though. The type of place where you could bring up a family. I didn't want that, or at least, I didn't want that at that point in time. I wanted something more,' Rose said.

This something more brought her to Sydney.

Of course, this wanting something more is also a post-modernist condition. A sense that we're all made for a far more exciting life. A celebrity-ness of sorts, or, at the very least, the 'good life'. Psychologist, social researcher and writer Hugh Mackay would say that the 'good life' as we understand it, in such times, is happiness. A virtually impossible goal. I would argue that we strive for personal success, and our notion of personal success is guided by a series of milestones, a narrative of sorts, that we need to fulfil.

As Rose indicated, 'I have this strange feeling, always, that my life has never really started. I'm 30 years old, and I still feel like I'm in this preliminary stage, waiting for my life to kick off. Perhaps I thought coming to Sydney would be that genesis? That things would start when I got here. But I still feel, well … not realised, I guess.'

Rose is incredibly articulate. It's obvious that she is educated, but also she has that notable skill of being able to communicate in an easily understandable way. She puts complex thoughts into relatable language. She connects with the listener quickly. And she's an extrovert. A powerful characteristic in a world fundamentally made for the right type of extrovert.

'I have seven brothers and sisters – you know, a very Catholic family. I'm the youngest. My brothers and sisters are all in relationships. They're either married or they have partners … most of them have kids, and homes and important jobs. You know, they have actual lives. I'm not quite there yet. I'm still waiting for that to happen.'

For all intents and purposes, Rose would seem like the type of person who has it together. She's highly educated, works in a large-scale advertising agency, in a high profile job, and lives in an affluent and incredibly beautiful part of the world.

I ask her why she feels like she hasn't made it, or her life hasn't started, or why her life isn't as worthy as the ones lived by her brother and sisters.

She pauses for a moment, and looks up – at this point we're on a Zoom call, it's the middle of the COVID-19 lockdown of 2020, and we're unable to meet in person. However, Zoom still gives you the sense of a person. The tone of their voice, their pauses, their expressions … the intangible prompts that go towards understanding how a person is thinking and feeling at a point in time.

Finally, she responds. Like most people, she doesn't respond to the question directly. But her answer signals a larger internal conflict – the feeling behind the response.

'You see, I don't really like my job. Bizarrely, it was kind of my dream job. When I studied communications, working in a big advertising agency in Sydney with huge brands – that was my dream. But now that I'm doing it, I work really long hours, I'm constantly anxious, under pressure – and I feel like I'm doing meaningless work.'

'What do you mean by meaningless work?' I ask.

'Well, it's not like I'm changing the world, you know? I'm not having an impact on people's lives. I'm selling people things they don't need. Like, it's empty work.'

'What would you do now if you could turn back the clock?'

'I think psychology. Having been through my own struggles … I think I could help people. If I could, I would go back and study psychology. But it's not really a viable option. I'd have to take time off work, do an undergrad – and you know, I just can't afford that.'

I nod.

'Is that what makes you feel like your life hasn't started? The job issue?'

'Yeah, to some degree. I don't like my job, I don't own my home. I rent my place with a couple of other girls. I'll never own a home the way things are going in Sydney … and, you know, I haven't met someone. I'm not in a relationship.'

'Do you think if you had met someone it would feel different?'

'Yeah, I suppose. I don't know. Sometimes I think if you don't meet the love of your life, it's kind of like your life hasn't started. And then other times I think ... who cares? So what if I don't meet someone. I have great friends. A fulfilling life. You know?'

I nod – even though this is a clear contradiction to what she had previously said. But you learn over the course of interviewing many people that they're filled with conflicting personal opinions, and sometimes those polar opposite, negating opinions sit side by side.

'Maybe if one of those things was in place then I would

feel more …' She searches for the right word, and then says, 'Solid.'

For Rose, without the purchased home, the right job, or the relationship, she feels ephemeral, intangible, not a realistic proposition. She hasn't met the critical milestones dictated by a broader cultural narrative.

'And is that why you're on a dating app?' I ask, bringing it back to the research.

'I suppose.'

'So, you're on the apps to meet the love of your life?'

'No!' She scoffs quickly.

'No?'

'I mean, sure, if I meet someone on the apps then that would be great … but I wouldn't say that's *why* I'm on the apps.'

'So, *why* are you on the apps?'

'I guess for a bit of fun … mostly to relieve the boredom. You know a bit of chitchat, or whatever.'

'Tell me about your journey on the apps. When did you start using them? What apps do you use? You know, a bit about your experience.'

'Okay… Well, I started using the apps when I was living in Canberra. In my early 20s, I'd say. Just because everyone was using them. But Canberra is a small place and you kind of know everyone there … so it didn't really work. I probably really started using them when I got to Sydney – you know, to meet new people as well.'

'And what apps do you use?'

'I started with Tinder, but it felt like it had had its day, and then Bumble, but I rarely got any responses on Bumble, and now Hinge, because it's more of a relationship app.'

'So, you didn't have any luck on Bumble?'

'Nope! I would message guys and they would never message back.'

'Because women have to message first on Bumble, right?'

'Yeah … that's right. Don't get me wrong, I would usually let guys make the first move, but on Bumble you have to, and I would literally get no responses.'

'That's interesting – you would usually let guys start the chat on apps?'

'Yeah – I guess, I'm a bit traditional like that. I think men should make the first move. But on Bumble you have to – and yeah, nothing.'

'Why, do you think?'

Long pause.

'I don't know, maybe deep down, men find it a bit

intimidating when a woman makes the first move.'

'Even today?'

'Yeah … I think so.'

'Okay – so you said you're on Hinge now because you said it's a relationship app, but before you said you're not really looking for a relationship.'

'I'm not really the hook-up type. I am looking for a relationship – but I just can't imagine finding it on an app. I know that's a funny thing to say, and everyone's like, apps are the place to meet someone … but it just seems so wrong to me.'

'What feels wrong about it?'

'I don't know … I guess my brothers and sisters all met people face-to-face – why am I the only sibling that has to meet someone on a dating app?'

'Okay … do you think you should meet someone face-to-face?'

'Yeah, I guess. I mean, you grow up watching all of these romantic comedies, and thinking your eyes are going to meet someone's across a room sort of thing – and that just never happens. I feel like I'm a bit of an old school romantic. My parents were high school sweethearts; they met when they were 16 at school, and then they've had this incredible relationship … they've built this family together. I was spoiled in that way – I thought something similar would happen to me, and then, well, it didn't.'

'And dating apps are a poor substitute?'

'Exactly! People are like – nobody meets face-to-face anymore, you need to be on a dating app, but I just feel like it's so desperate and strange.'

'What makes it strange?'

'It's like people are compressed in this strange way – into a couple of images and a bio – and you're supposed to make a call on that … and somehow it makes you incredibly judgemental. I look at men's profiles and if they're not tall, dark and handsome, I'm like, nup, you're out.'

'So, it makes you judgemental? You wouldn't act like that in real life?'

'Absolutely not! You know, when you meet people in real life, you hear the tone of their voice, the sound of their laugh … all those little bits and pieces that make someone … someone, I guess.'

'Okay, so what has your experience been like on Hinge?'

'Not great.'

'How so?'

'Well … at first it was like Bumble. I was getting virtually no matches, no direct messages. I'm there thinking, I'm a good-looking woman, with an education, a great job … what's this about?'

Indeed, Rose is what would be described according to heterosexual standards as good-looking. She has long dark hair, dark eyes, an arresting bone structure, a slender figure, and on all the occasions that we've interacted, she has presented in a well-dressed, fashionable manner. Impeccable even.

'So, what happened?'

'Well, I ended up showing my profile to some of my friends and they were like … you look super-high maintenance. You're way more chill. You need to fix this.'

'Interesting – so what made your first profile high maintenance?'

'I had all of these photos up of me going out … you know, dressed up, makeup done, hair done, that sort of thing. And I do like going out. So, I don't think it was a bad representation of myself. Also … I think, I only take photos when I'm out … it's not like I take photos of myself when I'm working out, or relaxing at home, you know?'

'So, it was just the photos that made you high maintenance?'

'Yeah. And in my bio I had, "Living a Champagne life on a beer budget" … and my friends were like – that has to go.'

'What was wrong with that?'

She laughs. 'I don't know! I thought it was funny. And I thought it was very true as well! But they thought it might convey that I was high maintenance! Which I'm absolutely not. I make my money, I spend my money. I'd also put down that I had a master's, and they said to get rid of that – makes you seem stuck up, and too smart.'

'Okay … so, too smart is also high maintenance?'

'Well, I don't know if it's high maintenance – but I guess it's intimidating.'

'Which is a problem?'

'I suppose.'

'So, what happened?'

'Well, I changed my profile. I added photos of me hiking in Canada, no makeup, and some of me at home, and left one "done-up" pic, and I changed my bio to a quote from that Liar Liar movie, with Jim Carey in it, something about the penny always being blue… And I started getting matches and chats.'

'Why did you use that quote?'

'I remembered that my brothers liked it – and thought

it would be the type of humour that appealed to men. Or made me seem, you know, chill and cool. The type of girl who cracks jokes and watches the footy.'

'You don't like the movie?'

'No … never watched it.'

'Okay … so, then you start getting matches once you changed your profile shots and bio. Was it a noticeable uplift?'

'Yeah, absolutely. At the start of the year my phone was pinging off the hook with notifications from dating apps.'

'Did you feel a bit weird about needing to represent yourself in a different way to get matches?'

'I guess, but it's such an artificial environment. It feels like a bit of a game, so I didn't feel too weird about it. It's not like that's how I am in real life or anything.'

'I see … so it's just to get more matches?'

'Yeah, I suppose.'

'And where to from there? Did any of them progress to dates or relationships?'

'Not really.' She laughs, and then looks sad. 'After I changed my profile we went into lockdown – then there was a lot of activity on dating apps. Like I said, my phone was just going wild – to the point where I had to turn notifications off. So many matches and chats, I felt like it was a second job almost. Sometimes I felt so overwhelmed just going back to my phone and finding all those messages – I didn't know where to start.'

'Would you say that you felt anxious about it?'

'Absolutely. It was kind of like that stress when you come back from a holiday and you have 15,000 emails in your inbox and you're like … I can't do this.'

'But nothing eventuated?'

'No. I mean, it's a bizarre experience. It's like the middle part of the experience is taken out. There is the original chitchat at the start of getting to know someone, top level, and then there's sex. There's nothing in between. There's not that getting to know a person, like if you were meeting someone in the office, for example. It's just not … right.'

'But you don't use the apps for hook-ups?'

'No way – it's so off brand for me.'

'What do you mean – it's off brand?'

'Oh, you know, I'm not the type of girl that just hooks up – I'm more the serious relationship type.'

'Okay. So, what's been going on for you during lockdown with the apps and romance?'

'Well, I went off the apps for a while because it was

just stressing me out too much; it's such a time waster, and I think it was making me feel more emotional about everything.'

'Why's that?'

'I think everything is amplified during Covid – I've never cried so much in my life, about anything. I feel like everything is standing still – I can't move forward with my life. My job, relationships, it's all stagnant. I'm 30, so this is a key year for me, in terms of moving things forward, and I just … I just can't because of Covid. It's taken a year from me – a key year in terms of…'

'Meeting someone?' I fill in.

'Maybe. I don't know, maybe.'

'So, you've had no interactions from a romantic perspective during this period?'

'No. After I went off the apps, I started texting with a guy I met last year and went on a date with. I met him on a dating app – and he was a bit older than me, in his forties, but still, you know, attractive, youngish. He'd never been married, no kids, worked in finance … he ticked all the boxes, but there was something creepy about him. I couldn't put my finger on it at the time. But then he started texting me during Covid, and I thought, why not? I'm not going to meet someone else, he's already someone I know, maybe I didn't give him a fair chance. We were texting for ages, but then it got weird. He started saying things to me like "Can I come around and fuck?" Out of the blue, in the middle of the day. And I'm like … no. But then he got really insistent, and he was saying weird things like, "I'll brush your hair and then we will fuck." I ignored him – and he sent all this crazy stuff about how I'd never have sex ever again because of Covid. So, I ended up blocking him. It actually really creeped me out, because he had my address and everything, because he'd dropped me off after that first date.'

'You were scared he would come to your place?'

'Yes and no. I mean, I live with two other girls, so it's not like I'm alone, but it did creep me out a bit.'

'I can imagine – did you think about reporting him?'

'I mean, to who, right?'

She has a fair point there.

'So, now where are you at with things romantically?'

'Well, I'm back on the apps. I do that all the time. I go on, nothing happens, I get frustrated, and then delete everything, and then I think … well, where am I going to meet someone now? And I go back on, and the cycle begins again. I haven't met anyone. But, you know, I have my flatmates, we're like a family. And we support each other … we laugh and cry together, we commiserate. I don't know where to with men. Maybe I'm one of those people who will never meet anyone. Maybe I'm just too difficult. Maybe I'm asking too much. Maybe other women would have entertained the brush and fuck idea? I don't know. I might just be too much.'

'You think you're too much in relationships?'

'Well, I've been told that before – I've been told that I'm high maintenance.'

'And what does that mean?'

'I guess, that I want…. That I want to be treated right. Like I should be. And, I suppose, in today's market that's just too much.'

8

Femmes fatales and feminists

'Out damn spot!'

Cries Lady Macbeth as she tries to wash her hands clean of the terrible crimes she's committed. One of the leading characters in William Shakespeare's *Macbeth*, the Lady goads her husband into committing regicide, after which he becomes the King of Scotland and she of course the Queen.

Goad is the correct word for her actions as recounted by Shakespeare. There's a violent disgust associated with interpreting them, and a certain inevitability – like she truly is the spike driving cattle towards their beastly end. She is the villain, the murderous traitor, even though Macbeth is the *actual person who perpetrates the crime*. You can feel a certain sadness when considering Macbeth, a kind of sympathy for his lost soul, but not so for Lady Macbeth – she is cast as the devil incarnate.

A regicide. Such villainy can only be *goaded* by a woman, and yet equally, can only be carried out by a powerful man.

Author Margaret Atwood calls out Lady Macbeth, amongst other female narrative protagonists, in her now famous 1994 speech, *The Spotty Handed Villainesses.* She discusses the duality that exists for women in narrative fiction – they are either very, very good or perfectly evil. There's no space between for women to be represented as complex and nuanced. However, as more women have become writers and authors this has changed – but how much so? To represent a woman as bad was to be inherently anti-feminist. This does little to progress women as conglomerates, mosaics – as inherently complicated and ever-evolving beings.

Villainy, as we see with Lady Macbeth, belongs in the empire of men, and those women who stray into the vicissitudes of such sin – murder, lust, pride etc. … well, they shall suffer a mad, mad end.

Like narrative fiction, there are often limited roles for women to fill socially, culturally, and romantically.

One might remember the 2022 *Married at First Sight* saga where Domenica was cast as the lusty villainess. In possession of a loud voice and feminist opinions, she held her mate to sexual account (why wasn't there more sex to be had? she demanded) as well as the rest of the men for their often sub-par behaviour. Then she came to loggerheads with Olivia, a pure-as-snow, WASP-like creature, who was always amenable to her male counterparts. The rivalry came to a head with the smashing of a glass (perpetrated by Domenica). And lo! Such an act of violence from the fairer sex. The piece de resistance was delivered when Olivia revealed that Domenica had an OnlyFans account and had been selling sexualised images for her own benefit. The majority of Domenica's cast mates quickly turned on her, Piggy-Lord-of-the-Flies-style, only to quickly recall that we were in the throes of a post-#metoo movement, and that they might be judged harshly by the Australian public.

Plot shift – the villainess and saint switch positions. Domenica is suddenly cast as the regal dove who stands for all of the things we believe to be good and progressive, and Olivia is cast as the vicious sinner. Again, no space between for any shade of grey or nuance; the only roles available are Madonna or Whore.

The men on the other hand continued sipping their beer, wondering when the women would turn more chill and less high maintenance.

The high maintenance woman is, of course, the villain of the piece. The woman with the heavy makeup, the woman with spiked heels. All indication of the wayward woman. After all, the Madonna would be plain of cheek, dressed in a modest gown, and her feet would be shod in flats. She would be naturally flawless.

As Italians would call her, she would be 'acqua e sapone'. Soap and water.

The femme fatale is the painted woman.

Ostensibly, the femme fatale *is* the villain. But she's also a model of female power, poise and intelligence: the femme fatale embodies Hollywood's contradictory attitudes towards ambitious women, and more broadly our contradictory attitudes towards powerful, ambitious, or should I say, high maintenance women.

The femme fatale, as seen in Hollywood, evolved over time on the silver screen and on the TV screen. She started with ethnically exoticised silent film vamps like Theda Bara and Pola Negri, progressed to classic film noir femmes fatales like Barbara Stanwyck in *Double Indemnity*, and went on to include postmodern revisions of the archetype in films like *Basic Instinct* and *Memento*.

The femme fatale brings discourses of female pleasure, power and violence to the fore.

Clever, no doubt. Ambitious, of course. Scheming, most definitely. But ultimately, about to suffer a very sticky end. And, we want these women to fall; *after all, they aspired to too much*.

They wanted too much.

They were too difficult.

Couldn't they just be more pleased with their lot in life?

Couldn't they be more – low maintenance?

Perhaps our strongest modern day Lady Macbeth is the one and only Kim Kardashian. Her ascent to fame some 20 years ago was ruthless to say the least. Accordingly, the media and contemporary culture have portrayed her as a wanton woman, a woman with no skills and no talent; nothing, in fact, to recommend herself other than a robust derriere, an ambitious 'momager' and that now infamous sex tape. Some 20 years later, she and her sisters remain at the top of the celebrity game, dictators within the fashion space, the language space, and even the female physique space. Like it or not, the Kardashians have been integral to our understanding of modern day culture, in particular, women's bodies.

It is hard to put the feminist movement in a neat, tidy box – but the concept of different 'waves' seems to help. Experts argue that 2017 was the midst of the fourth wave. It is mostly online and digital, where artists, celebrities and average social media users employ their bodies to make statements about race, class, gender, sexuality and bodily autonomy.

Thanks to their long-standing TV show, profitable business ventures and robust social media platforms, the Kardashian-Jenner family has an enormous digital media presence. The Kardashian-Jenner clan is 'unapologetically sex- and body-positive' and more trans-aware than most other celebrities – three characteristics that are staples of fourth-wave feminism.

Although many fourth-wave feminists would argue that the Kardashian-Jenner clan act as serious media influencers who share a semi-positive, feminist message with their viewers and followers, the Kardashians would argue otherwise, refusing to be pigeonholed under the title of feminist. Both

Kim and Kylie have avoided the 'F' title – as have many other women of their generation.

As popular culture, gender and sexuality writer Angelia McRobbie argues, this is no surprise. Feminism in the 1980s and 90s was shown in a certain ugly light: a burning of bras, repudiation of men, lesbianism, even. Feminism was distasteful. And instead a new kind of empowering women was introduced, exemplified by programs like *Sex and the City* and *Bridget Jones' Diary*. Women were cast as independent, hardworking, highly sexualised, but *not* feminists. Instead there was a sense that equality had been reached and that striving for feminism was no longer relevant. Women still wanted traditional roles; like Bridget Jones they just wanted to be happily married – they refused to meet the spinster-like end reserved for the banshee feminist.

Yes, the Kardashian-Jenners represent a strange brand of feminism. You could describe the Kardashian-Jenners as accidental feminists. Kris Jenner, the 'momager,' runs the show – quite literally. In addition to serving as an executive producer for their decade-long running TV show, she manages herself and her six children: Kim, Kourtney, Khloe, Kendall, Kylie and Rob. She is the matriarch and is responsible for the significant revenue this family has raked in over the past 10 years.

The family is centred around strong, independent women. Kim, Khloe and Kourtney Kardashian – the eldest three sisters – have faced constant criticism from the start of their careers about their curvy bodies and comfort with their sexuality. These women are fiercely independent. Though the world has watched them date, get married and have children, they make it clear that they do not depend on their significant others in any way, shape or form. Kendall and Kylie Jenner, the youngest sisters, now have flourishing careers and businesses of their own.

Rob, the single brother and son, has only recently come back into the spotlight following an absence because of body-image issues. It took his ex-girlfriend, Blac Chyna, to get him to return to the public eye. However, he has since retreated into the background again. Lastly, there is Caitlyn Jenner, formerly Bruce Jenner. Her transition, which began in 2015, was incredibly public, and her family never failed to support her as a woman. None of her children or stepchildren disowned her, and they all shared trans-accepting messages to their followers.[20] Their trans-inclusivity is questionable for many in the LGBTQIA community, but they have advocated enough to be considered trans-aware and trans-accepting.

Many people may argue that the Kardashian brand of feminism doesn't serve any woman; however, there is some merit in examining the power, and the fury which has sought to bury these women (and ironically made them, a consistent source of conversation). Their presence in media, and on the cultural scale is ubiquitous, almost unavoidable.

The Kardashian-Jenners are dominant on social media – their followers are in the millions. They can't go anywhere without a bodyguard, and their business products are in high demand. They have branded themselves as sexy women who do what they want, are not afraid of their sexuality, and practise self-love.

The Kardashian purview is so broad, it's hard to put an actual ring around its imprint. It's not just the television program, *Keeping Up With The Kardashians*, it's the spin-off programs from *Dash Dolls* to *I am Cait*, the magazine covers (hello, these ladies are now gracing the covers of *Vogue*), the truly omnipotent social media accounts (of which Kylie Jenner effectively owns the lion's share), the emoji lines (or kimojis), the apps (so you can follow their lives even more carefully), the video games, perfumes, handbags and lipstick lines... Not to mention the children's wear line, Kardashian Kids.

You can't swing an ample derriere without it making contact with a Kardashian product. And we, the Kardashian consumers, continue to feverishly consume.

The signs and symbols of the Kardashian world have made their entry into contemporary culture. People are wearing eye shadow before midday, fake eyelashes have become du jour, extensive lip lining on point, hair extensions, booties... Yes, plentiful derrieres are now the way of the day. We have become emblems of the appropriated world of Kardashian Kulture.

Professor of functional and comparative genomics Neil Hall coined a term, the 'Kardashian Index' (or K-index), to describe people whose 'overblown public profile' results in undue weight being placed on their views. He outlines the K-index as a 'measure of discrepancy between a scientist's social media profile and publication record based on the direct comparison of numbers of citations and Twitter followers'. In other words, the more famous you are, the more people care about what you have to say, even if you're not an expert. The paper is armed with a mean theory and an algorithm to match.[21]

The Kardashians are incredibly public. Historically, men have had privileges in the public domain, for example in business and government, and women have been relegated to the private space of the home and the family. Accordingly, women have had limited voice in shifting the policies and ways of life which impact them.

Men were seen to be rational, intellectual, factual, and women were seen as the opposite: emotional, focussed on the body as opposed to the mind. This is a Cartesian read of the mind/body duality, and went towards arguing the split between public and private life for men and women. Women, after all, were too emotional and not rational enough to participate in the largely scientific space which was the factual landscape of the public domain.

Across the last 200 years these spaces have shifted, penetrated and become more malleable – with women permeating the public domain in a more comprehensive way.

However, one could also argue that women are still not as present in the public domain as men. Even in 2022, the Australian federal election saw the independent 'teal' women's contingency storm the male-dominated political space.

In addition, women have been heavily policed within the social media space. Arguably, women dominate social media, particularly visual platforms like Instagram. At the same time, women have been the greatest victims of trolling and abuse within the online space.

The internet has allowed for technological, economic and social progress on a scale previously thought unimaginable. However, when it comes to accessibility and safety for girls and women there is still a long way to go.

One recent study by Plan International, a humanitarian organisation concerned with equality for girls and children's rights, found 58 per cent of the female respondents between 15 and 25 had been the victim of some form of online harassment or abuse, which included derogatory language, targeted humiliation, body shaming and threats of sexual violence.[22]

The creator of the Web, Sir Tim Berners-Lee, highlights this issue as part of a 'growing crisis' affecting girls and women on the internet. As well as the issue of users feeling safe, there are greater implications for online misogyny that requires creative and large-scale solutions. Head of Plan International Birgitte Albrectsen feels it limits girls' 'freedom of expression' and 'damages their ability to be seen, heard and become leaders›. Those who do make it into power have to contend with a much greater quantity of abuse, in a phenomenon now being categorised as violence against women in politics (VAWP). This includes attempts to threaten, silence or intimidate female politicians online – something which particularly affects younger women and women of colour.

However, even when users aren't presenting themselves as female, and therefore painting a target on their back, they still have to navigate the wealth of sexist content on social media. If sexist attitudes are abundant in playgrounds and in workplaces then you can easily imagine how on the internet, the unpoliced wild west, they are practically unavoidable. This affects even those who are not deliberately posing as women online. When a woman faces abuse merely for having an opinion, or appearing on media, it contributes to a culture of intimidation that deters spectating women from appearing in any form on the internet, let alone speaking up about sexism – still a contentious subject among many.

It is this intimidation which polices women in the public domain of the internet.

Yet, the Kardashians stand as powerful and incredibly visible characters within this domain.

The spotty handed villainess, the femme fatale, the clever and ambitious woman – they are all the high maintenance woman. They defy the need to be perceived as chill, cool, quiet. They do not sit by the sidelines, cheering on their companion. Instead, they are public with their ambitions, with their sexiness, with their intellect – and as a result they are policed. Policed via media scrutiny and ridicule and policed on public forums like social media.

Amelia's story in context

Amelia's story and experience on dating apps highlighted some key issues in the high maintenance women's space. She would class herself as a low-maintenance, chill, relaxed girl. And she worked hard to maintain and perpetuate this narrative, at times at her own romantic and intimate peril. In remaining chill and not establishing parameters for her relationship, she set no expectations, and eventually found herself in a situation where her intimate partner was 'talking' (having another intimate relationship) with someone else. She tended to lower her expectations, and accepted a number of bad behaviours without articulating the issue.

In addition, she was quite sure that despite her 'low maintenance' ways, the majority of guys would still pick the 'pretty' girl. Again, here, there was no safe territory. Chill, relaxed, pretty, low maintenance, high maintenance – they were all critiqued. She was forced to navigate an incredibly slender line, which led to online and personal identity management. She couldn't really be herself nor could she ask for the things that she required in the relationship to make herself feel safe and loved.

Amelia also raised another interesting paradigm: that of women policing other women in the online environment. Like many of the women in focus groups, she used other women, and groups of friends, to check her profile, write her bio, check her images, and so on.

Feminist scholar Akane Kanai draws on the work of Lauren Berlant, a scholar and cultural theorist, to discuss 'best friend culture' within digital intimate publics. Kanai describes how women come to police each other's practices, creating profiles based on fantasies of feminine sameness. Knowledge, labour and skill are required to craft generic selves through which attachments to a normative girlfriend sameness may be fostered.[23] Meaning that to participate within these digital intimate spaces (like dating apps, or Instagram) women had to know the language and behaviour which is endorsed, both visually and narrative-wise. I would argue that commonly within these spaces women act in 'low maintenance ways' or self-deprecating ways, reinforcing issues of anxiety, mental health and a feeling of not being enough.

There is a policing of identity which occurs within the women's space, which weeds out uber-confident women – alpha women, high maintenance women, sexualised women – who are perceived as arrogant, whorish, not displaying the characteristics of low self-esteem accepted and encouraged by today's society. Women need to be a work in progress, constantly working on themselves, identifying their flaws, to be acceptable. The opposite of your high maintenance femme fatale – the Kim Kardashians of this world.

Ironically, these women are also held up as examples of beauty, sexiness and empowerment. In a double-handed movement, women are told they need to tote the expensive handbag to demonstrate success, and have physical enhancements done (breast, bum and face) to be sexually attractive, yet are vilified at the same time for being 'plastic', 'fake', 'up themselves', 'not authentic,' 'not real' – all with the aim of meeting the ever-growing expectations of men, who require the 'chill model' in a relationship.

In addition, such women, who are desirable and visible, are policed by men, through displays of technologically facilitated violence – for example, the dick pic. When Amelia seized her sexuality and sought just sex, she received constant requests for nudes, and unsolicited dick pics. She was labelled and treated as the whore.

She was told to make herself small – and, yes, to disappear completely from the online space.

So, she became invisible.

9

Lily: Trapped between the spotty handed villainess and the chill girl

Lily is in her late 20s and a talent agent. She recently moved from Melbourne to Sydney for work. She's smart, lively, and declares herself to be a feminist. She lives in Marrickville with a close friend, and she is looking for love. However, she doesn't use dating apps just for love, she uses them to make new friends, and for sex.

'Initially, I thought dating apps were a bit of a joke. I never thought I'd have to use dating apps to *actually meet* someone. I'm quite extroverted so I meet men in person all the time – at work, getting a coffee, on the bus … wherever. But I got to the point where all the men I met, who I was interested in, they weren't interested in me. So, then I got onto Bumble and Tinder, more as an experiment. I'd also just moved from Melbourne to Sydney, and I guess it was a good way to meet people and get to know the city.'

'And why did you move?'

'I was offered a new job and it was a good opportunity, but also I think I'd gotten really comfortable with my life in Melbourne – and I sort of wanted to push myself out of my comfort zone. Meet different people, see a different part of the world.'

'And how did it go with the dating apps and Sydney?'

'I met lots of guys and went on a lot of dates, but none of them really clicked. They were mostly friendships, no chemistry. And then I met a guy on … I think it was Hinge. I had started using Hinge because my boss was like, Hinge is where it's at. Anyway, he was this tradie, funny guy. I wouldn't say necessarily my type, but we had this amazing chat online. We had planned to go on a date that weekend, and all week we were talking. Every time my phone pinged I felt like I was a school kid, and would blush a bit. Anyway, he took me on an offbeat date where we went to this ritzy auction, and sat down the back and had a laugh about the bids. Like real rom-com sort of stuff. Then we had a fantastic dinner, and I thought … geez, I really like this guy. I told myself, Lily don't sleep with him on the first date, that gets you nowhere – but I did, because we just had this amazing connection. Like crazy chemistry, love match sort of thing. After that, he's planned the next date, and we're texting all week – nothing changes, this amazing connection continues.

'We're planning to go out on Saturday night, but he hasn't given me the specific details yet … and then I stop getting messages on Saturday. This is weird because he's a serial texter, always sending messages. Also, I know he's got an Apple iWatch and is always checking it and getting messages … so, I know he's seen the messages that I've sent him.

'But I still think there's a reason to it all. It's not until about 8pm in the evening that I realise I've been ghosted, and I'm there sobbing into a tub of ice cream and watching *A Star is Born*. My housemate turns up and asked what I was crying about. How bad Lady Gaga's acting is? And I'm like, no, I've been ghosted.

'The worst thing is – I was obsessed with this guy for weeks. So, sometimes, I would think … what if he's dead or something, and I'll never know? Eventually, I got to this point where I had to figure it out, and I had his full name, so I looked him up on social media – and discovered that he was alive and well … and even worse, one of the jokes I had made on our date, he had used that as a caption to a selfie on Instagram not long after he ghosted me.'

'That's pretty terrible, isn't it? What do you think happened there?'

'I don't know. But this sort of thing happens all the time. After that, I was like … I'm done with dating. You know, when I was in my early 20s, I had a really casual attitude towards men. I'd hook up with them, like them, but not get so personally involved, and I wanted to go back to that sort of sentiment. I wanted to get rid of that desperate, I-can't-make-any-relationship-work kind of vibe.'

'And what did you do?'

'Well, I started this intimacy experiment, and it was all about hooking up, being empowered again from a sexuality perspective.'

'Okay, so tell me about how that worked for you.'

'I set up a new profile on Tinder, and basically it was just body shots. You know, really sexual images of bum and boobs, and I had this bio "Here for a good time, not a long time", and basically explicitly said I was looking for no-strings-attached hook-ups. I won't lie, I'm a sexual person, I like a hook-up. So, I thought I'd go back to basics. I started scheduling in guys, like one in the morning, one in the night. Sometimes I'd go through two a day, sometimes none, and in the course of 30 days, I basically had sex with about 40 men, and I got my confidence back.'

'And did you find that the men respected the parameters that you had set up?'

'Yeah, absolutely. I ended up getting them to come to my house. Because it's just a hook-up, so why should I go out of my way for them? It's not going to progress. There was one guy, who looked nothing like his profile, and his breath smelt … and I was like, no, I'm sorry, I just can't, and told him to leave. He begged a bit, but eventually he left.'

'You weren't concerned about your personal safety, what with them coming to your house?'

'No. I mean, no. They were harmless. I live with a dude. Not in the slightest.'

'Do you think any of them could have progressed to being more than a hook-up?'

'Absolutely not. I mean they're there for a hook-up and so are you – nothing more. It's just sex. I mean, the first guy I hooked up with, I remember we had this really nice chat afterwards, and I did think, he could have been something more if it hadn't started like that. But it did.'

'And why don't you think things can progress if the hook-up kicks things off?'

'I don't know. Because you've agreed to those terms and that's it. Also, once you've been perceived in that sort of light, I don't think you can reverse out of it.'

'Do you mean the kind of girl that someone hooks up with?'

'Yeah, I guess. You go into that category.'

'And did it work out for you? Did you feel empowered?'

'Yeah … I guess. I definitely got out of my relationship funk, and eventually I met someone on Hinge. Because I had kept the other profile going. You've got to be in it to win it – you know, find the relationship.'

'And you met someone?'

'Yeah, I did. We've been together for a couple of months now, and we've had the conversation, so I've removed my hook-up profile.'

'I see.'

'You know, can I say, I know I said a moment ago I felt empowered, but I don't think I was empowered at all. I'm sort of pissed off that I have to use dating apps now to actually meet someone. No-one introduces anyone, no-one chats to people anymore … it's like we've all become lazy, or we've been forced into this digital relationship environment, which is so judgemental … and so fake. I mean sure, I probably made it work, or did I? I actually don't know.'

10

Love and finances – a history of the gold-digger

White, Western culture represents finding love as the pinnacle of our life stories. The notion that love is the fulcrum to our existence, or the precursor to a life well led, is deeply entrenched in our cultural narrative. The idea that meeting the love of our life is a critical life milestone is reinforced through film, theatre, literature and art. On the opposite end of the spectrum, singledom is perceived as some sort of loss, a waste, even a personal failure. We feel sorry for our single friends. We swamp them with helpful anecdotes and joyful slogans that their day will come too.

We ask them questions like: 'Are you seeing anyone?' 'Anyone special for you at the moment?' Or just simply: 'Dating?'

We placate them with: 'It will happen for you.' 'It will happen when you're not looking.'

Always with an earnest, kind, empathetic look on our faces. Those of us in a relationship may feel a level of jealousy; possibly our relationship is far from perfect, perhaps even deeply flawed. We might even be questioning the need for that relationship on a daily basis. But *it is a relationship* – hence we're validated by broader society. We might envy the freedom of our single friends; their capacity to watch whatever they like of an evening on television, have great sex with a stranger, and simply not have to engage in the multitude of boring household tasks and minutiae of life with a significant other.

Yes, there is a degree of envy involved, but also an equal pinch of pity. We know, secretly, that they've failed.

The reality here is that being alone is *not* okay. Because the world is not built for single people. It's made for couples. It's made for coupled lives, and families. The heterosexual narrative is so present and so overbearing that we are all completely and utterly across it, and yet it operates in subversive ways – so much so that we're not aware we're participating in it or guided by it.

For example, often in my focus groups and interviews, I heard the words: 'I wasn't looking for a relationship, I was so happy being single … but then this happened.'

Or:

'I wanted to not get serious, date multiple people, not get attached, but then I met [insert name] and everything changed.'

We lie even to ourselves – we twist the truth. We indicate that we would have liked to live wild, free, sexually liberal and personally independent lives, and yet something draws us back – somehow, we drop into the monogamous narrative, so quickly, so easily, so comfortably.

The narrative … well, there it is: dating, sex, falling in love, moving in, maybe purchasing a dog (a Groodle – a perfect example of the dog required in a heterosexual romance) and, of course, the proposal, so ubiquitously documented on social media, and so forth … the marriage, the house and children. This is the life story we believe we should lead. When we fall short of these constitutive events we question our worth, our capacity to be functioning individuals.

We're even cast aside. Because society provides a narrative for lovers and duos; it doesn't provide a story for those outside of that model.

But where has this 'coupled' ideal come from?

You could go back to Plato – perhaps not the genesis of this tale but certainly the early perpetrator and discussant of the idea.

In the beginning, humans were androgynous. So says Aristophanes in his orgastic account of the origins of love in Plato's *Symposium*. Humans had two faces, four hands, four legs, and both sex organs. They got around via cartwheeling.

Zeus was threatened, and split them down the middle. If, however, the humans continued to pose a threat, Zeus promised to cut them again, and if they weren't sufficiently weakened to make a second cut – 'and they'll have to make their way on one leg, hopping!'

The severed humans were indeed distressed, Aristophanes says.

> *[Each] one longed for its other half, and so they would throw their arms about each other, weaving themselves together, wanting to grow together.*

Zeus took pity on them and turned their sex organs to the front, so they could at very least be one briefly.

Contained in this fantastical text is Aristophanes infamous speech on love.

For Aristophanes, humans look for satisfaction in all the wrong places. These false lures include material goods, power and fame, which leads to an empty life.

Christian philosophers, led by Augustine, accepted this diagnosis and added a theological twist. Pursuit of material goods is evidence of the Fall, and symptomatic of our sinful nature.

Humans seek to satisfy desire in worldly things, Augustine says, but are doomed because we bear a kernel of the infinite within us. Thus, finite things cannot fulfil. We are made in the image of God, and our infinite desire can only be satisfied by the infinite nature of God.

In the 17th century, French philosopher Blaise Pascal offered an account of this wound within in a more secular way. He claimed that the source of our sins and vices lay in our inability to sit still, be alone with ourselves, and ponder the unknowable.

We seek out troublesome diversions like war, inebriation or gambling to preoccupy the mind and block out distressing thoughts that seep in: perhaps we are alone in the universe – perhaps we are adrift on this tiny rock, in an infinite expanse of space and time, with no friendly forces looking down on us.

The wound of our nature is the existential condition, Pascal suggests: thanks to the utter uncertainty of our situation, which no science can answer or resolve, we perpetually teeter on the brink of anxiety – or despair.

The notion of the 'soulmate' implies that there is but one person in the universe who is your match, one person in creation who completes you – whom you will recognise in a flash of lightning.

What if in your search for true love, you cast about waiting or expecting to be starstruck – in vain? What if there isn't a perfect partner that you're waiting for?

Alternately, what if you dive into a relationship, marriage even, expecting the lustre and satiation to endure, but it does not, and gives way to … everyday life, where the ordinary questions and doubts and dissatisfactions of life re-emerge and linger?

In his book *Modern Romance*,[24] actor and comedian Aziz Ansari tells of a wedding he attended that could have been staged by Aristophanes himself:

> *The vows ... were powerful. They were saying the most remarkable things about each other. Things like, 'You are a prism that takes the light of life and turns it into a rainbow'.*

The vows, Ansari explains, were so exultant, so lofty and transcendent, that 'four different couples broke up, supposedly because didn't feel they had the love that was expressed in those vows'.[25]

And yet more and more we seek this kind of love; this epic, light-my-world-on-fire kind of a love. We look for a partner who satisfies all of our needs: sexual, emotional and intellectual, and yet we want this love to never be comprised. For lust never to burn out, for the butterflies to continue, and when they do not, we question that connection. We seek help. And finally we ask, is this the soulmate I was told existed, made only for me?

We might then choose to split the union apart, and begin the search again.

This quest for an exceptional love was professed by Plato, but for centuries, instead love was more of a compact – where goods and services were bartered and exchanged.

Men and women (any type of same-sex union was seen as perverse in the majority of the white, Western world) were often coupled off by family members or extended family, according to a variety of diverse rituals, and based on rank and status. For example, affluent members of society were expected to be matched with equally affluent people, and so forth. Women were often traded almost as chattel, to sweeten deals, or even to secure the family fortune. Funds were exchanged via a dowry, for example. Little attention was paid to their desires and needs, or their concerns in relation to love, soulmates and suitors. Perhaps this practice was the beginning of women being labelled as 'gold-diggers'.

Women were (and still are) exchanged between men – fathers to suitors – and marked as a result by the man's name.[26] This meant a woman had no choice; the 'my body, my choice' slogan would have fallen on deaf ears, and even today, it is still a rebellious claim. Women are still expected to exist within certain romantic and sexual landscapes, as we have seen in the case studies of Amelia, Kristina, Rose and Lily. A woman is still expected to take a man's name when they marry (with the exceptions of nations like Mexico and Italy which have legislated that a woman should maintain her surname). It is still customary or 'traditional' for a man to ask a woman's father for his permission for her hand in marriage.

The birth of the Victorian era ushered in ideas of love as we know it in a modern way; however, even at this point there was a rational, consumer trade element in the equation. This concept was made famous through the novels of Jane Austen, whose heroines desire a 'big' love but also a good fiscal match. After all, Lizzy only really fell for Mr Darcy after she had inspected the hallowed grounds of Pemberley and discovered the girth of his wealth, which went beyond description. Passionate love featured prominently in Austen's novels, but it was often the women who abandoned their sense of propriety and were carried away with the emotion, leading to them suffering the consequences of a difficult life.

This concept is perhaps best evidenced through Marianne Dashwood in *Sense and Sensibility*. Marianne represents the opposite side of the coin to her highly rational sister, Elinor (Sense). Instead, Marianne embraces spontaneity, excessive sensibility, love of nature and romantic idealism. She weeps dramatically when their family must depart from 'dear, dear Norland', and later in the book, she exclaims:

> *Oh! with what transporting sensations have I formerly seen them fall! How have I delighted, as I walked, to*

> *see them driven in showers about me by the wind! What feelings have they, the season, the air altogether inspired! Now there is no one to regard them. They are seen only as a nuisance, swept hastily off, and driven as much as possible from the sight.*[27]

To which the cooler Elinor quietly replies, 'It is not everyone who has your passion for dead leaves.'

And later when Marianne hears Sir John Middleton's account of John Willoughby, her eyes sparkle, and she says,

> *That is what I like; that is what a young man ought to be. Whatever be his pursuits, his eagerness in them should know no moderation, and leave him no sense of fatigue.*[28]

When Marianne is helped by the dashing Willoughby, she falls deeply and sincerely in love with him, abandoning all society's conventions and ignoring her sister's rational warnings that her impulsive behaviour leaves her open to gossip and innuendo. His painful spurning of her, and the shocking discovery of his dissipated character, finally causes her to recognise her misjudgement of him. She acts exactly as she feels, thus making herself and everyone around her miserable when Willoughby leaves her. Elinor, on the other hand, keeps the secret of Edward's prior engagement to another in her quiet, thoughtful way (Edward being her preferred suitor).

Marianne also exposes herself to that terrible thing, 'society's censure', often mentioned in Austen's novels. A woman was always expected to guard her propriety. To be transported by sentiment was to be giddy, silly, emotional – to be all the worst traits that pertained to a woman; all the things that kept women out of the public domain and facilitated men their entry because they were rational, intellectual and factual. This public/private and emotional/rational divide was evident in the Victorian era, as was the notion that romantic endeavours, compacts and proposals needed to be witnessed.

Love was conducted privately, but always under supervision. Victorian women were chaperoned as they were not allowed to be alone with a man until they were engaged. A woman was never to go anywhere alone with a gentleman without her mother's permission. A woman was never to go out with a gentleman late at night. In fact, it was considered extremely impolite for a gentleman to stay late at a woman's home. A gentleman could only call on a lady with her permission. When saying goodnight, the girl was never to go further than the parlour door; instead, a servant would see her suitor out.

Church socials and holiday dances would have been considered suitable places to meet a potential partner, and glamorous galas or balls were common. But just because a gentleman had been introduced to a lady for the purpose of dancing did not mean that he could assume to speak to her at another time or place. This would be improper! If a gentleman met a lady he wished to become better acquainted with, he was to make subtle inquiries to find a mutual friend who could introduce him. One thing that was permitted at social events was flirting. Subtle flirting techniques included using various personal accessories such as fans, parasols and gloves to convey messages of interest or disinterest. Once formally introduced, a gentleman could offer to walk a young lady home by presenting her with a card that asked if he could be her escort. The woman could then weigh her offers and present her own card to the gentleman she liked best.

Women were still traded, to some degree – exchanged for the security of wealth – and men were viewed as a way to secure a good life for a woman. Men married to protect their family's interests. As Austen wrote in *Pride and Prejudice*[29]: 'It is a truth universally acknowledged, that a single man in possession of a good fortune, must be in want of a wife.'

In modern day white, Western culture, love moved away from the closed doors of parlours and out into the world of newly minted malls. In *Labor of Love: The Invention of Dating*, author Moira Weigel writes that dating as we know it came about in the late 19th century, when there was a shift from private to public courtships.[30]

Academics like Professor Eva Illouz from the Ecole des Hautes Etudes en Sciences Sociales in Paris write that the birth of modern day capitalism, and consumerism, ushered in a different type of dating that was highly public and commercial.[31]

Romantic encounters moved from cloistered exchanges in the home, under the supervision of family and friends, to public and commercial spaces like restaurants, bars and the movies. This public shift meant that love came to be characterised by the consumer marketplace. The signs, symbols and milestones of dating intertwined with consumption and the visual economy. Austen-esque courtship may have ended, but it was replaced by another set of rules which were highly visible.

The visual economy applies to being 'seen out' and engaging in the romantic consumer spectacle. Today it applies to the sharing of these visual consumer romantic signposts via social platforms like Instagram, Facebook and Snapchat. Here, in the digital domain, the language of love, the visual and the marketplace becomes truly entangled. You might be familiar with the plethora of hashtags available for you to categorise your romantic image and relationship: #engagement #engagementring #wedding #diamondring #diamonds #official #bride #groom – just to name a few.

Many would argue that the world of dating apps continues and amplifies this visual love economy, as users are asked to make a split-second visual decision on a potential match based on a profile pic. Professor Illouz says about online dating apps, 'What the internet apps do is that they enable you to see, for the first time in history, the market of possible partners.'[32] Or at least those the algorithm will allow you to see. Individuals are available in a marketplace of consumption – with transactions made similar to an UberEats scenario – and are 'bought' based on a good/bad visual decision-making process.

This is a particularly bleak view of the dating app realm

and the world of relationships. Certainly, there is an intrinsic link between love, the commercial and the visual economy; however, this link is not 'new'. The market, love and the economy of visibility have always been intermingled.

Besides first dates in bars and restaurants, and other romantic consumer signposts, like the 'we're-getting-serious weekend away', love has become coded by a series of highly commercial symbols – none more recognisable then the diamond ring. Anthropologists date the ring practice back to the Roman custom (which originated in the 2nd century) of wives wearing rings attached to small keys indicating ownership, but the idea of the diamond ring really hit its stride in the late 1930s.

Recent research traces the ubiquity of the diamond ring as a symbol of engagement to the discovery of massive diamond mines in South Africa in the late 19th century, which flooded world markets with diamonds. The story goes that British businessmen operating the South African diamond mines recognised that only by maintaining the fiction that diamonds were scarce and valuable could they protect their investment.[33]

In 1888, they launched a South Africa-based cartel, De Beer Consolidated Mines, extending the control of all facets of the diamond trade. In 1938. New York advertising agency N.W. Ayers was recruited to drive consumers' understanding of the link between eternal love and the diamond ring. Ayer's pitch articulated how movie idols, the paragons of romance for the mass audience, would be given diamonds to use as their symbols of indestructible love.

In addition, the agency suggested offering stories and society photographs to selected magazines and newspapers to reinforce the link between diamonds and romance. Stories would stress the size of diamonds that celebrities presented to their loved ones, and photographs would conspicuously show the glittering stone on the hands of well-known women. Ayers also planned for fashion designers to talk on radio about the 'trend towards diamonds'.

The Australian wedding industry contributes around $3.6 billion annually to the local economy. There were 56,124 wedding businesses operating in Australia in 2019.[34]According to *Money Smart*, the average wedding costs $36,000 (AUD), and 82 per cent of Aussie singles dip into their savings for their weddings.[35] COVID-19 would likely have changed these figures as couples sought to postpone weddings or operate within restrictions on guest numbers. Despite this, the tight link between dating and the marketplace cannot be ignored.

Here the consumer marketplace becomes truly entrenched in the language of love, and the language of the 'gold-digger' starts to slip in.

And perhaps there is truth to some of these claims. White, Western women have been told to define their identity through things and milestones. The intermingling of these two elements is not even discreet; indeed it is overt. As Carrie Bradshaw, from *Sex in the City*, announces in her third person dialogue, in one of the *Sex and the City* movie spin-offs, she moved to New York City like many women, in search of, 'Labels and Love'.[36] Having gotten the knack of maxing out her credit card on expensive purchases like Fendi bags and Manolo Blahnik shoes she moves on to the next category, love. And, of course, her key suitor, 'Big', puts together the two elements of romantic love that are very much required in a modern relationship: not only does he light Carrie's world on fire but he is also incredibly wealthy; wealthy enough to support her somewhat fiscally challenged lifestyle.

Women in romantic fiction and pop culture are defined by their love stories, but similarly by capital and labels.

A girl in contemporary fiction often becomes a woman by acquiring things. The clothes she is wearing, the bag she is toting – these are all emblems of who she is. Look no further than hit programs like *Gossip Girl* to see this labelled entry into womanhood articulated. This is not to say that contemporary heroines are not nuanced and diverse, or that there are no other ways to portray being a girl or a woman; however, the predominant narrative tends to lend itself towards love and capital. Evidenced through the incredibly popular franchise of *The Real Housewives of X*, women, post-marriage, are expected to engage in a world of expensive, capital spectacle – and this is perceived as success.

Subsequent series like HBO's *Girls*, and *Fleabag*, provided different ways for women and girls to represent themselves. However, even here the worlds of love and personal identity were linked with consumption in strange ways. As Jia Tolentino wrote in The *New Yorker*:

> *I also don't think* Girls *demands identification as much as satirizes it. The main characters are never more ridiculous than when they are explaining the way they see themselves – in one of Marnie's funniest moments, at her infelicitous wedding, she described her aesthetic as*

> *'Ralph Lauren meets Joni Mitchell,' with a 'nod to my cultural heritage, which is white Christian woman.' The fruitlessness of endlessly fine-tuning your self-image—of frantically trying to echolocate your personhood against someone else's story, real or fictional—is baked into every episode of the show. This is particularly clear in the scant number of episodes, just a dozen or so over six seasons, in which Hannah, Marnie, Jessa, and Shoshanna have appeared as an ensemble. In these episodes, the characters' independent narcissism generally becomes unwieldy: the four of them go to the North Fork with competing ideas of a good weekend, and their trivial preferences become statements of purpose – ammunition for a fight about who they are.'*[37]

The idea that women have to be defined against a certain pre-existing schema, much of which relies on capital and labels, is continued in a subversive way. So, perhaps it is not so strange that the idea of the gold-digger or the 'high maintenance woman' (the modern equivalent of the gold-digger) continues.

As the digital world has pervaded our relationship narrative, through dating apps but also through social media, the signs and symbols of love and identity have been incorporated into how we represent ourselves via these online applications. Perhaps initially this was embodied by the Facebook relationship status update, which was an early noughties (now almost prehistoric) way of sharing news about a new relationship – and, yes, the idea that you had indeed 'made it'. Heterosexual women demanded that nonchalant partners updated their Facebook status, and men who did the same were often told they were 'the woman' in the relationship.

However, the days of speedily updating your Facebook status the moment a new relationship is made official are long gone, replaced by a new form of social media relationship documentation – the 'soft' or 'hard' launch. Social media oversharing has become a commonplace occurrence – and the trend of PR-speak creeping into the realm of relationships and intimacy is growing. The soft and hard launch trend combines both.

Love, labour and the consumer marketplace have always been intrinsically linked, and the evolution of 'public dating' via social media documentation is worthy of investigation. The internet, and platforms like Instagram and TikTok, give rise to a new visual language of relationship milestones, a language which is highly nuanced, and interlaced with gender scripts and cultural capital.

The relatively new celebrity-led trend of soft or hard launching a relationship (predominately) on Instagram or TikTok involves users subtly ('soft') or explicitly ('hard') revealing a new relationship via a photograph or video and accompanying caption.

A soft launch might involve an image of two hands clasped together – think the Kourtney Kardashian/Travis intimacy reveal. A hard launch might feature the lucky couple locking lips (think Jennifer Lopez and Ben Affleck). Zendaya and Tom Holland's Instagram soft launch was widely reported and speculated on – the use of the phrase 'my Spider-man' a subtle choice.

This trend, made famous by two of the greatest Instagram lovers and documenters, actress Megan Fox and musician Machine Gun Kelly, has ushered in a new age of seemingly unhinged, cringeworthy lovers' posts on Instagram by ordinary people.

It's a way for media and tabloids to report on celebrity relationships, but it's also become a widely used tactic for regular people to broadcast to families, friends and followers what's happening in their intimate lives.

If you're looking to dive right into the new trend of social media relationship documentation, a word of caution: you're entering a maelstrom of complex relationship milestones. You might want to follow one of the many 'Insta-official' internet guides which handily outline the best way to launch and document your relationship on social media. You might also want to consider in advance what to do with the content if the relationship falls apart – will it be an erasure of the evidence? Or a public statement announcing the end of the relationship? The digital dating breadcrumbs left behind require attention.

These days we have to be aware that we have romantic social stocks. That these exist as examples of our social worth. Use the Instagram-official blueprint correctly and your social stocks will likely soar. Take as evidence Kourtney Kardashian's Instagram account, which grew by 44 million in 2021 following her relationship Insta-reveal.

The milestone of finding a life partner is seen as a critical one which continues to hold cultural and social relevance. When we narrativise our lives there are a number of acceptable pathways available, and the romantic union is a highly recognisable one which has developed a certain visual formula within the social media space.

Is there room for subversion in this highly scripted domain? For living an intimacy outside of the realm of super-saccharine and contrived Instagram moments? My research would indicate that in the space of dating and the digital domain there are disruptions, but there are also continuities. This means new dating behaviours emerge in the digital space, but for the most part dating narratives remain the same – for example, a romantic proclivity for finding *the one*. Often these continuities reflect an update from an IRL (in real life) space to the digital realm.

The 'soft' or 'hard' launch of a relationship could be seen as an extension of a key courtship milestone – becoming official, building on and surpassing traditional milestones like meeting the friends or family or anniversaries. However, the focus on the self as a brand, and the self-in-love as the premium brand, requires our vigilance.

The world was witness to Kourtney Kardashian's spectacular wedding to Travis Barker in Portofino, Italy. The relationship has unfolded to a watching crowd, all seemingly via social media. It would seem that the relationship and its milestone events were orchestrated for social media. From the first declaration of love, through to the moments of their modern-day romantic courtship, to the proposal, which was captured for the Kardashian hit TV series and social media, to the wedding, a Gothic-romantic extravaganza brought to you by Dolce and Gabbana. And while we watched on – engrossed, obsessed, disgusted and perhaps vaguely jealous – it was hard not to see how this event had all of the ingredients of the love/intimacy/fiscal du jour relationship.

Indeed, the ingredients are so intermingled now that it's hard to separate them; they've come together as a soup of sorts.

So, it's difficult to imagine or pinpoint why the discussion around the 'high maintenance woman' continues, especially given the current state of affairs in which love, intimacy, labour and finances are intrinsically entwined. Or why women are to blame for such a state of affairs, given that their male counterparts seem to happily participate in the spectacle. White, Western culture continues to indicate that men are the drivers of the romantic bargain. For example, the proposal is still a male prerogative.

The role of tradition in both personal lives and intimate partnerships in contemporary societies is disputed. Individualisation theories have been criticised for overestimating 'de-traditionalisation' — how traditions become increasingly irrelevant for people who reflexively create their own biographies. In modern societies, where traditions are chosen and not imposed, wedding traditions are likely to be subjected to critical reflection to varying degrees; some may be taken for granted, other elements are examined, adjusted or rejected. But how much here is actually scrutinised? How many of us can formulate a separate and authentic narrative in the domain of romantic love and intimacy?

Sociology Barbara Risman's gender structure framework conceptualises gender as a stratification system operating simultaneously in multiple processes at three dimensions of the gender structure — individual, interactional and institutional/macro — including both material and cultural elements.[38] The gender structure constrains choices, but individual action includes reflexivity and actors' interpretations of their situation, and responses may either reinforce or challenge existing structures. People's choices thus reshape gender structures over time.

According to the gender structure framework, at the *institutional* or macro level, organisational structures (including formal and informal regulations) and ideologies shape gender relations.[39] Most laws and policies have become gender neutral in Western societies, but dominant cultural ideologies about what it means to be a woman, or a man, may remain. Ideologies shape the possibilities for change – they influence behaviour and choice at the individual level, expectations at the interactional level, and uphold unequal structures at the institutional level. However, ideologies are complex, and different aspects can change independently of each other. At the *interactional* level, individuals encounter expectations about gendered behaviour from partners and others. At this level, cultural stereotypes and taken-for-granted assumptions are important. Resistance to gendered expectations are always possible but may be accompanied by substantial costs; reactions to non-conformists depend on what is considered appropriate at any moment of history. At the *individual* level, cultural ideologies are internalised into gendered identities and gendered ways of interpreting the social world, shaping people's self-perceptions and their ideas about themselves as gendered.

Besides being rooted in gender inequality, the common denominator of the three wedding conventions – the male marriage proposal, the gendered division of wedding planning and women's name change – is their puzzling continuation in institutions, social interactions and individual self-perceptions.

Despite having a capacity to choose differently, or even, for many, having more progressive ideologies when it comes to gender and gender relationships, men still decide how romantic relationships progress, and we celebrate these milestones. Type into any Instagram search #engagement or #shesaidyes and you'll see a myriad of images of elaborate proposals, some of which might cost as much as the wedding itself. Helicopter jaunts to spectacular locations, engagement rings the size of golf balls and, of course, the ever-present image of a smiling couple, side by side, her holding up her hand in triumph, wearing the engagement win.

Standard, textbook, heterosexual narrative. And yet, we celebrate this, consistently. It even raises our social stocks.

To some degree then, men buy into this elaborate love/fiscal affair. They participate … and yet, the high maintenance woman is still derided. It begs the question, is the high maintenance woman really about finance? Is the issue that she is expensive? Or is this a far deeper question?

Nikesh, who was a participant in one of my focus groups, is an example of a man who thought that some women were too high maintenance and too expensive, and that this behaviour was detectable via a dating app profile. Interestingly, he was educated, progressive, and one could even say a feminist, and yet …

11

Interview with Nikesh

Nikesh is a 27-year-old Sri Lankan-Lebanese-Australian man living in Parramatta. He has a double degree and master's and is an entrepreneur. He is also a part-time DJ. He lives with his parents and is looking for love, a connection and hook-ups. He is humorous and exuberant, but Covid has grounded him to some degree.

'How has Covid been treating your love life, Nikesh?'

'Not well … not well. I would say that I'm a face-to-face kind of guy. I have far less success on the dating apps. So, you can probably say that the core part of my game is no longer available.'

'Okay, so why do you think that is? Why do you think you have more luck in real life?'

'I don't know. I can hazard to guess that I'm more of an acquired taste. If I'm in town, at work, and I see a cute girl on the coffee line, I'll start some chitchat, crack some jokes, and sometimes, I walk away with her number. I wouldn't say all the time, not even half the time, but I have a nice flattering way about me, and you know I'm funny in a quirky kind of a way – and girls like that ... They don't get approached often anymore. So, if it's done in the right way, it's flattering. But if I'm online … it's like virtually nothing.'

'Do you think you just don't translate well online?'

'Absolutely. I don't translate well online. I would say that the online environment is for your uber-attractive people. I'm not that attractive, so I have to rely on my other charms. Also, I'm brown.'

On Zoom, he throws up his arms to demonstrate that his final words should be self-evident, obvious, a fait accompli.

I find myself saying, 'What do you mean by this?'

'Well, you know, dating apps are a white people's game. They're not for brown people.'

It's the first time I've encountered a statement like this, and the first time I've even let my mind stray into this terrain; a space where systematic racism occurs on dating apps. Sexual racism even.

'I'm still not following …'

He sighs. 'People like me, who are brown, and look like Muslims or whatever, we're not attractive in the white people's marketplace, and especially not in a space where people are making fast decisions.'

'This is the first time I've come across this concept … although I have read about it – it just hasn't surfaced in my research yet.'

'Well, I'm assuming most of the people in your research are white. Or that the "ethnic" people in your research are women – because they're like fetishised. You know, the whole concept of Asian women and all that. I guess it's harder for brown men.'

'Okay, so tell me what your usual experience is like on dating apps and how it's changed.'

'My usual experience is not a lot happens. I live in Parramatta so I have a radius around the Parramatta area, and usually it's the same faces and not a lot of matches.'

'And do you find that disheartening or off-putting?'

'Yeah, absolutely. But because I usually work in the city and also do DJing gigs I meet a lot of people in person, so it's less concerning.'

'And what about COVID-19?'

'Well, I guess there were positives to Covid, in that there were more people on the apps. All of a sudden there were all these new faces, so there were more options. But you can't really meet up or anything because we're in lockdown.'

'Would you say you were getting more matches?'

'Yeah, definitely. Not a huge number, but there was definitely an uplift. I did notice something else as well …'

'What's that?'

'Well, I'm not sure if I'm supposed to say this … it's a bit sexual.'

'Go ahead – you can say whatever you like in this format.'

'Well, I just noticed there was more women looking for a hook-up, and just a hook-up. It was like they got a little hornier.'

'I see. Why, do you think?'

'I don't know. Usually I get virtually no-one interested in a hook-up, and recently there's been a couple of girls who say, hey, come to my house or whatever. It's interesting.'

'And have you been to any of these hook-ups?'

'No. I mean, obviously I've been tempted. But I do live with my parents and they're in their 60s. My dad has underlying health conditions, so it's not like I want to bring Covid home for the sake of a hook-up. It's just not worth it.'

'And what type of women do you look for on a dating app?'

'It's not like I really want a relationship or anything, but I am open to having a relationship. I want to meet someone that I have a connection with. But I guess I'm open to something long-term or short-term, or even just a hook-up, obviously.'

'So, what's the type of woman you would swipe right on?'

'Well, I wouldn't say there's a type. But I guess, someone with a sense of humour. I have a quirky sense of humour, and I like to have someone who is similar, or gets my jokes, or we can bounce things around. Someone who I can have a good chat with. The DM chat is always a good indicator of having chemistry with someone. I want someone I can talk to – I don't want to spend time with someone who is a bit vacant, if you know what I mean. And obviously there's got to be a level of attraction.'

'How do you tell these things from an app? Profiles are a couple of photographs and limited content, really, from a written perspective, so what prompts are you looking for?'

'Look, to be honest, there are a lot of pretty girls on apps, right? Don't get me wrong. Super-done-up, the big lips and eyelashes, and hair, and amazing bodies … and they're hot, and they're the type of girl you'd probably want to hook up with. But it's too much. Super-high maintenance. It's not the type of girl that I want to spend a longer period of time with. So, yeah, they're the type of women I would usually swipe no to.'

'What makes you think they're not the type of woman you would like to be in a longer-term relationship with?'

'Well, I just look at them and think, how expensive would they be to upkeep? I just can't afford that. I'm not a rich dude. I couldn't keep a woman like that happy. And then I think, is this the type of woman I want to introduce to my parents? Also, I can just sense they would want too much, you know? They'd have these massive expectations on everything … and I just don't want to deal with that. I need someone who's more easy-going, down to earth. You know, a chill girl. Not someone who's going to be up in my face all the time about appearances. Also, not to draw out the race card or anything, but my parents are stricter South-

Asian, Middle-Eastern types, so I can't bring someone like that home. They wouldn't be happy.'

'So, would you look to date within your ethnic mix?'

'No, absolutely not. Within the Sri Lankan and Lebanese communities, in a particular area, you know virtually everyone and you know all the girls as well, and again, they're a particular type of girl. They're fairly conservative. I'm not conservative. I don't want to meet someone, settle down, put a ring on their finger, and then buy a house and have kids – and that's what's expected in the community. I want to travel and do interesting things and have interesting experiences. This is not what would happen if I ended up with someone from within the community. I feel terrible saying this, but they're pretty closed minded to a lot of stuff.'

'Okay, right. So, if you're looking for someone quirky and smart and open-minded, how do you tell this from a profile? It seems like a difficult conclusion to draw.'

'It is. The thing about apps is that they make you really judgemental, and you have to group them together based on things to do with their appearance. There's probably women in the mix who look really high maintenance but are actually smart and funny and whatever – but it's just impossible to figure that out when you're online, you just have to go with the general look of that person. So, yeah, I'd make the decision on appearance. I'd be lying to you if I said I looked at the bio and made a decision from there. After we've matched, yes, absolutely I'd check the bio, and then you know get a vibe from the DM chat. I can't stand typos or major grammatical errors or anything like that, or blatant racism in the chat or closed-minded views, so that all goes towards making a decision.'

'Have you met up with anyone during Covid?'

'No. I've chatted with a few girls online who were really nice, but it's kind of fizzled … because I guess it's the uncertainty. Are we going to be in lockdown for three months or six months or a year? How long before we actually get to meet? You know, I could spend six months investing time in a person, and then we meet and there's no chemistry. There's online chemistry and then there's in-person chemistry. There's a difference…'

'How do you mean?'

'You can have great chat with someone online, and then you meet them and there's no sexual attraction or physicality to it. So, it's a waste of time. I've wasted six months talking to someone for no reason.'

'Are you still on the apps now?'

'I go on and off. Sometimes I'm like, there's no point here, and then I'm at home, working from home, eating dinner with my parents, and I'm like, fuck, I've got to do something else here. It's a combination of boredom and desperation, and I'll go back on, and then … the cycle happens again.'

'I see. And do you have hope for your romantic or intimate endeavours moving forward?'

'Yeah, I suppose. There's someone out there for everyone, or so they say. It's not like I'm Robinson Crusoe here. We're all stuck together. So, yeah, post Covid, definitely.'

12

Difficult women: Intelligent, successful and career driven

There was so much nuance in Nikesh's words, and contradiction. Of course, hidden in this mix was the very hard truth that marginalised communities – in this case, people from a racially diverse background – were stigmatised in the online environment. There is a certain covert sexual racism which goes on via dating apps that is rarely acknowledged. This ostracism of particular people is something I deal with in Chapter 13 as well as the notion of the Aussie bloke.

But, alongside this was the articulation of the high maintenance woman by Nikesh, who was both othered and othering – and importantly, these two things happen routinely at the same time. For Nikesh, the high maintenance woman was entangled with the pornification of women, a culture of sexualisation of the female form, physical enhancements, finance, worth and difficulty. He remarked that such women would be too much work. What would they take to upkeep? And be happy? Would they be chill enough?

This idea of not being chill, or not being cool – returns us to our discussion about Gillian Flynn's concept of the 'cool girl'.

In 2022 I was invited to speak on the Triple J program *The Hook-Up*, hosted by Dee Salmin, about my research findings. Dee also hosts a podcast titled *The Not So Chill Girl*, which speaks to a similar concept as detailed in my findings: that women who aren't 'chill' are unlikely to get the guy. This not-so-chill element could manifest in many ways, from not being up for sex or certain sexual situations, to having what is perceived as complex eating habits, to an in-depth beauty routine, or even tough or challenging ideas. Essentially, the non-chill girl is a real person, with real sensitivities and nuances that are simply too difficult for men to deal with. Instead of creating space and a pathway for men to walk through life with ease, the non-chill girl has her own life and ideas, and this is perceived as 'difficult'.

Dee's podcast has garnered a huge following.

In this interview, Dee was looking to examine the idea of high maintenance. Through *The Hook-Up*'s Instagram page, Dee asked followers a number of questions, including if women had ever felt that they had represented themselves as too smart, or too successful, or too difficult, or too high maintenance in the online environment and as a result not received matches, and if they had ever felt the need to 'dumb down their profile' to get matches.

The response was overwhelming. Dee received hundreds of messages from women who changed their job titles on their profile, or used different images to seem less successful, clever or ambitious. She also received responses from men who confirmed the notion that the high maintenance woman was just 'too much'.

One of the most curious case studies which emerged from her mini-Instagram focus group was the story of Caroline, an aerospace engineer. Here is Caroline's story, plus a summary of some of Dee's findings.[40]

She's an aerospace engineer doing her PhD. She loves fashion and nice clothes. Her hobbies include fixing vintage cars and bikes, traveling, being a bit of a foodie and going out to cocktail bars with friends. She's bloody smart, and absolutely gorgeous. And she shows all of this on her dating app profile.

*You're probably thinking, f*ck you, Caroline! You must have so many matches and go on so many dates, I may as well delete my profile! Well well well, you'll be shocked to find out, Caroline doesn't get a single match. Like ever.*

It was actually getting her down so much, she dm'd us on our Instagram @triplejthehookup to get some advice on why this might be happening and what she should do.

She was confused. We were confused.

'I think I started off with "aerospace engineer" on my profile. And then more recently, I've put "PhD in energy harvesting on aircraft", and zero matches.'

Caroline realised it might be her job, so she decided to take it off her profile.

'I've changed all of my prompts to just stupid, funny things that have nothing to do with me. And all of my pictures are just photos with friends and I'm not particularly showing off in any respect.

'The rate of my matches has increased a lot. And I just don't know why I have to lie.'

Lots of 'successful' women aren't getting matches

This isn't just a one-off experience. When we posted about Caroline's story on Instagram, and so many other women (swiping for guys) got in touch with their similar experiences:

> *I'm a lawyer and I had to take that off my profile because I wasn't getting matched, or when I did get matched, I was getting asked for free legal advice.*
>
> *When I was 23, I bought my first house and I was quite excited about it and proud of it. So, I put the picture of me in front of the sold sign as the first picture on Tinder. And just a dramatic drop almost immediately in the amount of matches I was getting.*
>
> *As a PhD with a master's I had the same problem. Changed it to student and I was fine.*
>
> *Yes! I took off that I have a business and changed it to hairdresser and it completely changed.*
>
> *I used to have my course, Mechatronics Engineering, on my profile and got no matches then changed it to a barista and they came flooding in.*
>
> *Absolutely can relate to this! I am a doctor and when I*

> *was on Tinder it made a massive difference if I had it on my bio or not as to the number and type of matches I would get.*

Excuse me, hetero dudes, what's going on?

Turns out the patriarchy, gender assumptions, toxic masculinity etc. etc. etc. plays a huge part here.

We had a lot of hetero guys share their experiences and thoughts:

> *In general, guys are thinking what can I bring to the table? It's more of a self-confidence self-worth thing. We're taught that our value comes from what we can provide. We're thinking why would this amazing woman settle for me?*
>
> *Man's perspective here ... if the woman has more direction in her life than the man, as demonstrated with her degree and career this would be a turn off for that man.*
>
> *I am a male doctor and I used to actively seek high achieving intelligent females because we could get along on the same level. I think many men feel threatened and insecure in themselves so it makes them afraid to date these successful women.*

Guys in society are expected to provide a bit and then it's very hard to get away from that feeling.

Het man... first thing that comes to my mind is this girl sounds like she'd be working 10h a day 6 days a week and would not have time for a relationship.

I wouldn't swipe left on Caroline because it seems like a fake profile.

Caroline has priced herself out of the dating market.

It needs to be noted that there were also PLENTY of dudes who said that Caroline sounded like the girl of their dreams and they'd swipe right on her in a heartbeat. But where are they, if she's not getting matches?

As demonstrated through Dee's findings the concept of high maintenance stretched to women who were intelligent, successful and career driven. There was irony in some of the responses – the woman who had put a photo of her own home up, for example. This would seemingly indicate that this woman had her finances together, that she wouldn't require someone to 'upkeep her', that she wouldn't be seen as 'too expensive'. Similarly, the women with lucrative careers. Yet they were still perceived as too high maintenance, too difficult – and ultimately undateable.

The men's responses were equally disturbing – here ideas of patriarchy were indeed strong. Men expected to be 'providers' (but confoundingly, also didn't want to be providers); they thought that a woman as successful as Caroline would imply a 'fake' profile. The idea that Caroline had 'priced' herself out of the market spoke to the economic value of love and intimacy. In the romance stakes, Caroline was simply too expensive.

In the obscurity and anonymity of the digital domain, men were happy to flag their fragile egos. As one suggested, it was a self-confidence or self-worth issue. Again, women were told to make themselves feel smaller so that their male counterpart could feel more reassured.

If you grew up in the 1990s, 2000s and beyond, you were likely told that women could do anything. Study, travel, ascend to the highest echelons of government and all the rest. But what that rhetoric did not prepare women for was that, in response to displays of female strength, many men would reveal themselves to be as fragile as eggshells. Plenty of men had no interest whatsoever in seeing women in any sphere but that of the home. With institutional barriers removed (arguably in biased ways), the only recourse left to these men was to harass women back into a sphere of silent, compliant domesticity.

This policing of behaviour is seen overtly through the bullying of women in the online environment, whether through a dick pic or violent, misogynistic commentary.

Journalist Jennifer Wright wrote in 2019 in *Harper's Bazaar*:[41]

> *In 2014, Amanda Hess wrote about how, when she was on vacation, a man started a Twitter accounted dedicated to harassing her with messages like 'Happy to say we live in the same state. Im looking you up, and when I find you, im going to rape you and remove your head.' Hess was a sex and dating writer, but this happened to women in every sphere. As Hess noted, similar comments were directed to Alyssa Royse, a sex and relationships blogger, for saying that she hated The Dark Knight: 'you are clearly retarded, i hope someone shoots then rapes you.' To Kathy Sierra, a technology writer, for blogging about software, coding, and design: 'i hope someone slits your throat and cums down your gob.'*

This policing extends to quieter, less overt displays – like swiping left on a successful woman, educating women in a soft tone that they need to dumb themselves down to get a man. They need to stop articulating their education, success, their financial assets. The implication is that women should be small. They need to be pretty but not too physically attractive. They should be silent. They shouldn't challenge men on an intellectual or success level. And they most definitely should not be difficult.

This rhetoric is dangerous. It teaches women around the world, and distressingly, the next generation that they need to play into a male stereotype of what a woman should be – and that's smaller, and less than. That they should disappear into space and essentially become invisible.

There is no safe space for women. You can choose to remove the title of your education and job from your profile and substitute it with 'student', or delete the picture of that house you worked so hard to build like some of the women on Dee's podcast, but there will always be criticism. And then you risk being criticised for not being enough. Not smart enough, successful enough, financially viable, sexy enough or pretty enough.

Yes, there is no safe terrain. Women are forced to navigate an impossible world of identity management. A space where they cannot exist without criticism.

The only way they'll escape the criticism is if they are – Invisible.

13

Online covert marginalisation

Leo

Leo is a 30-year-old, Chinese-Malaysian-Australian man living in Sydney. He was born in Campbelltown but moved to Sydney in his early 20s after he completed a communications degree. He lives in Darlinghurst, Sydney's gay capital, and is an openly queer man. He has a successful role in one of the largest tech companies in Silicon Valley as the communications director for Asia Pacific.

Leo is looking for love, intimacy and hook-ups. He uses

Grindr, Tinder and Hinge.

'So, tell me, you use a couple of different apps, is your profile the same across all of them?'

'Yeah, absolutely the same. To be honest, I sometimes wonder why I use the three of them because it's kind of the same people across all three apps. But I do think Hinge is a little bit more forgiving – it's more about people wanting to make a genuine connection, but Grindr, in particular, tends to be a lot more cutthroat.'

'And what do you mean by cutthroat?'

'Well, it's very much about your appearance. It's all white dudes with their abs out, in underpants … it's very … vapid, which is a little bit like what Sydney gay culture is like.'

'Tell me about Sydney gay culture.'

'It's a very small pool of people. Most of us know each other. It is cliquey and very appearance orientated. There is a certain type of gay man that has more romantic success.'

'And what would that type of man be like?'

'The Aussie bloke type. Kind of like the gay Chris Hemsworth. There's a certain idea of what's masc. – masculine, I mean – in the gay space, and yeah, a masc. guy is preferred.'

'And what's a masc. guy?'

'He's usually white, very muscular, deep voice … almost an updated version of the stereotypical Aussie bloke, but one that fucks men.'

'A deep voice as well?'

'Oh, yeah, 100 per cent. I have quite a gay voice; it's a little high pitched, and I laugh a lot, and am fairly flamboyant, and that's not on trend in the gay community … it's seen as too feminine. So, sometimes I'll try to hide my voice. I'll make it sound lower on a first date so that I seem more masculine … that sort of thing.'

'Does that make you feel uncomfortable?'

'Of course, there's nothing comfortable about it. I feel like a fraud. But, you know, I'm Asian, so there's no getting around that "feminine" idea.'

'So, an Asian man is considered more feminine?'

Yeah, absolutely. I don't have body hair, and I'm leaner. I guess there's just this idea that Asian men are more subservient. That we're bottoms … in everything.' He laughs.

'Would you say Asian men are undesirable in the community?'

'Yes! So undesirable. This is one of the reasons why I don't like using dating apps – I can't deal with the full-on racism.

In person, people are a little more tactful, but online, that's all gone.'

'So, what type of stuff goes on?'

'It's very common for men to have on their profile – 'No Asians, just a preference'. Very common. And when I see that sort of stuff it really ... kills me. When I moved to Sydney I thought I would be living my own personal *Sex and the City*. Instead, I was introduced to this wild environment where nobody wanted to date Asians. I'm from Western Sydney, from an Asian community, so this kind of white world was so foreign to me.'

'It's common to have 'No Asians, just a preference' on profiles?'

'Yes! It's one of the reasons I go off Grindr or Tinder. It's definitely not a thing on Hinge. But it's certainly still a vibe. I probably get one match a week, or less, so even if people aren't directly saying it, they're thinking it ... Asians are either ostracised or fetishised. You know how these white men go to these crazy rice queen festivals in Asia, where it's 200 Asian men to one seedy white guy? They're like vultures. It's actually really disturbing, and yeah, it gets me down.'

'So, do you go off the apps as a result?'

'All the time. I'll spend a couple of months on there, and

then the behaviour is too much for me to handle, and I go off them, swear off them, and then a couple of months later I'm back on. In a place like Sydney you can still meet someone in person. The prejudices are still there if you meet someone in person, but you know I'm a funny guy, I'm fairly charismatic, so I think I can get around it. But online it's like hitting a brick wall. Then sometimes there's a lull and I get desperate and think, everyone is online, I need to go back on … and the merry-go-round starts again.'

'Do you ever feel like you have to change your persona to fit the Aussie bloke stereotype?'

'Yes. But you know at the end of the day I'm still Asian. I can't change that. I'll never change that. That's the reality of it. I can't discard my ethnicity. But I do things like upload pictures where I look more muscular, where I'm wearing less flamboyant shirts. Where I'm having beers with mates … because beers are a very bloke thing. I do try to somehow squeeze into that persona, even though I'm quite aware it's never going to happen.'

'And have you had any luck on the dating apps? Have you met anyone significant?'

'No. I've met hook-ups, and I'm up for a hook-up. I'm happy with a hook-up. But sometimes people want something more. I wonder if I'm going to meet someone myself and have an actual relationship – and these days it seems less and less likely – but then I get to thinking, is this a heterosexual ideal? Do I want this – or is it just a heterosexual ideal of what I should want? The relationship.'

'Well, this is a good question.'

'You know, the heterosexuals, they colonise everything.' He laughs again. 'But I do want a relationship.' He laughs again.

'And are you hopeful about that?'

'No, absolutely not.'

Michael Zhang: Slow Love

In August 2020, I started a podcast series called *Slow Love* with the production company Contento. Our aim was to document love during Covid times. At this stage my in-field data collection was complete; however, I still had a number of questions which didn't fit into the size and scale of my PhD. One of them was, what happens to intimacies forged during the pandemic when lockdown ends? Were they just as enduring as relationships developed IRL (in real life) and pre-COVID-19? One of the key findings in this research was that COVID-19 and the use of dating apps didn't necessarily engender the right conditions for developing an intimacy. Whether it was the uncertainty of when a face-to-face meeting would be permitted, a lack of animation and movement, the lack of romantic narratives, the labour of self-presentation, or the jagged love cycle – intimacies for these participants were stymied.

The other reason I chose to start the podcast was the subject matter within my thesis was so important, and so timely – it seemed that for most participants the importance of connecting and creating an intimacy was paramount, particularly during a Covid world. The stories that participants shared with me were so passionate, intense and unabridged. They retold components of their intimate lives which I believe they had never told others. There were tears, and even shame.

Shame about being ghosted. About having to use a dating app to develop an intimacy. About not having enough matches. About receiving or requesting nudes. About never having met a significant other. About wanting things that were perceived to be pedestrian, like a romantic other.

It struck me that most of the participants who came to the in-depth interviews came with a desire to unburden themselves. I almost felt like a priest receiving confessors, except I couldn't confer a pardon or offer three Hail Marys as penance. This didn't seem to matter; they came, simply to talk about love, sex and intimacy, and to be listened to.

It occurred to me that the avenues to discuss such things are limited. In 2022, real discussions about intimacy are still lacking. The podcast gave people the opportunity to provide their intimate stories in an unabridged fashion. Many chose to go under pseudonyms, others relished in detailing their secrets and disclosing their identities.

In November 2020, the podcast was top 5 in the Australian podcast charts, after we handed over the mic to an escort. She took on the role of host and interviewed one of her clients. The interview was an insight into the world of sex work during COVID-19, a topic which went mostly undiscussed by the media at the time. When news.com.au picked up on the podcast, we hit an all-time record of number 4 on the charts, directly behind the Michelle Obama podcast.

We ran the *Slow Love* podcast for just under 12 months, concluding after we failed to secure funding. However, those involved in the project concurred that it was an incredibly worthwhile one, which compiled COVID-19 stories of intimacy, similar to the Berlin love letter archive (only on a smaller scale!).

One story which was captured on the podcast seemed to summarise my research: the shifts in intimacy during COVID-19, the casual racism of dating apps, the labour of self-presentation, romantic narratives, the final question – what happened to intimacies forged during this curious period of time?

Michael Zhang is an Australian man with a Chinese background. He lives in Melbourne, and his parents own a chain of bargain stores. Michael has been looking for love for some time – he is close to 30, and it's his parents' expectations that he should meet someone and settle down. However, Michael's not completely convinced about the idea of 'settling down', and has progressive views which vary from wanting to find a wife and monogamous relationship, to entering an open relationship. He seems to flit between these ideas somewhat ambivalently. Michael uses multiple apps including Tinder and Bumble. However, he thinks that these apps are made for 'white' audiences, and he indicates that it's well known within the Asian communities that Asian men in particular don't do well on 'mainstream' apps. In the past he has laboured to create a more 'white' profile, but eventually gave up. He notes that Asian men have no market on dating apps, but

Asian women are often fetishised in the dating app space.

Michael starts using an 'Asian' romantic app called Tan Tan during the pandemic, and he meets a woman of his age from a Filipino background. He has met her previously IRL, and this seems to speed up the intimacy between them. They meet discreetly during Covid, and not long afterwards they move in together. There are pragmatic reasons to this moving in. She was looking for a place – and he wanted the company during Covid-iso. Michael seems ambivalent about whether or not they're suited romantically. He concludes that they'll just have to 'wait and see'. He indicates that their relationship has gone through a compressor. He also muses that only a couple of months in, they find themselves seated in front of the television in their pyjamas at 10am eating cereal. It's almost as though the fun, getting-to-know-you stage of their relationship, when you go to bars, dinners and festivals, has been removed and replaced with the mundanity of a relationship that has been in motion for a couple of years.

I ask him whether he thinks the relationship will last post-Covid lockdown. He says it's a good question. After a pause he indicates that they'll likely need to re-test the relationship in a Covid-free world. He says that he has never seen his girlfriend in a social scene, never introduced her face to face to his friends. He reflects that the dynamic between them is a Covid-lockdown specific one, which might not work in the outside world. But he's willing to give it a go. There is, he says, something between them.

Post-Covid lockdown, I check in with Michael on a second podcast, and he has since broken up with his girlfriend. It simply didn't work out, he says. They rushed it during Covid, and came to dislike each other and the routine they fell into. They didn't even get the chance to test the relationship on the other side; once Covid-lockdown ended they went their separate ways.

The course of Michael's relationship reflected the Covid lockdown experience. The Covid accordion time compressor was present. Michael met his match online, but the relationship was accelerated as they previously knew each other. However, because they moved in together quickly, and 'settled down' because of Covid lockdown, the pair removed critical relationship milestones that can be expected in building a romantic relationship, for example, dinner dates, meeting the friends, meeting the family, and so on.

Previously, in Chapter 10, I mentioned Professor Eva Illouz from the Ecole des Hautes Etudes en Sciences

Sociales in Paris, who argues that love has been colonised by consumption, and in the mid-20th century moved from the confines of private courting to the public, consumer spaces of dinners, movies, bars, etc.[42] She also states that these spaces are highly visible, and that love requires this visibility to indeed exist. Both of these elements were removed for Michael and his match, as well as the romantic milestones which we have come to learn are vital to the progression of participants' relationships within this research. It was almost as though these punctuations (milestones) and visibility were even more required within the Covid world, where time was flattened, and life inertia was experienced. The romantic milestones would have removed the sense that he was otherwise wasting time in this relationship.

Online marginalisation/racism and sexism

In my research, the high maintenance woman concept emerged as a way of policing women, intellectually, emotionally, physically and even visually; however, it soon became clear that there was a sort of covert sexual racism and sexism apparent on dating apps. This was conducted so quietly that it was considered the norm rather than the exception. Just another factor to the dating app experience. Michael and Leo didn't necessarily call out this sexual racism, nor were they shocked that dating apps weren't safe space for Asian men, they simply accepted it as part of being on dating apps.

From behind the anonymity of the digital world, users were able to make their racist or sexist desires apparent, whether that meant adding lines in their profile like, 'No Asian men, just a preference', or simply swiping passed brown and Asian men. This sexual racism was not only directed towards Asian and brown men, although both Michael and Nikesh did remark there was a 'fetishisation' of Asian women online (a reverse kind of sexual racism), but as indicated by Dr Bronwyn Carlson's research into Aboriginal use of dating apps, it is true of many ethnically diverse and Indigenous groups.[43] She writes that Aboriginal women often received racist and sexually violent messages on dating apps. Many Aboriginal women within her research chose not to disclose that they were Aboriginal within their profiles, or selected images which made them look less Aboriginal.

Conversely, Carlson also found that some Aboriginal women found dating apps to be empowering spaces, where they blocked out white men, and a continued 'sexual colonisation'. As some Aboriginal women discussed within her research, white male rape and violence towards

Aboriginal women in colonial Australia was rarely discussed, and was continued today in subversive ways. Dating apps provided a way for Aboriginal women to taken control of this narrative.

However, overall, dating apps proved to be a largely judgemental space, where users fell into habits of categorising people according to physical and ethnic characteristics. Seemingly flippant and even humorous comments hid all sorts of physical and racial prejudices:

'I like them tall, dark and handsome. If they're not six foot, I swipe left.'

Or

'I like Aussie blokes, big, tall, muscular, you know ... The funny type.'

And although it can be argued that the dating app space is conducive to these sorts of behaviours because of the anonymity and the need to make quick decisions (it's not a getting-to-know-you kind of space; it encourages immediate categorisation), dating apps can also only be seen as a reflection of modern society in Australia – and the behaviours that are alive and well all over the country in relation to love, sex, intimacy and race.

14

Celeste: The type of narrative that never surfaces

Celeste is 35 years of age, she has a three-year-old, a lucrative career, and a long-term partner. She owns her home in the inner city, and appears from an outsider's perspective to have it all. She has suffered since her late teens from a chronic illness, which has led to her being often hospitalised, unwell, and with significant scarring on her stomach. She has recently gone through a physical transformation – she has redone her breasts, added significant filler to her face, had botox, hair extensions and eyelash extensions. I have interviewed Celeste before and she strikes me as a completely different person. The woman I had known only six months ago was somewhat pale, drawn, incredibly slender, and indeed rather pretty, in a non-enhanced type of way.

This change strikes me as curious, particularly as she had always described herself in a certain light – in the background, the passionate hard worker who would prefer not to be seen. I'm not sure why this doesn't strike me as analogous to these changes – but the shift reflects a certain desire to be noticed, potentially through a male lens, even though today it would be cast as a sign of 'empowerment'.

I know that Celeste is having intimacy issues with her partner. They haven't had sex for over a year, and she finds this lack of sexual contact disturbing, but also she's left to desire more. She, too, is a sexual being, and this coldness from his end has meant she has sought physical intimacy outside of her relationship.

'So, tell me,' I begin, 'have you been using dating apps to meet men for sex?'

'No,' she laughs. 'I was on the dating apps briefly, but I found men very strange and aggressive there … especially when you tell them you're married and looking for sex.'

'How do you mean?'

'Just really provocative in their language, like, do you want to fuck? Or wanting nudes … it felt gross.'

'Did you meet up with any of them?'

'No. A friend of mine told me this story about how she met a guy on a dating app for sex – went to his house, and then he tried to choke her during sex, and wanted to cum in her face. It was pretty awful … she was shaken from it. I just didn't want to have an experience like that.'

'Have you been having sex with your husband?'

'No – we haven't had sex for over a year now. He's just not interested in it anymore. He's become … asexual almost. But as I mentioned last time, I've had a talk to him and I still have needs and desire, and he's okay with me meeting up with someone for sex, as long as it's not a relationship, as long as there aren't feelings. We love each other, you know? We're just not having sex … which is a separate thing. And we want to stay together – so I guess we're looking for other ways to make this work.'

I nod. I've heard this before from Celeste, and indeed it's not uncommon for a long-term partnership to run out of intimacy.

'Last time we talked about you potentially seeing male

escorts. Have you explored that?'

She laughs. 'Yeah, I've seen a few.' Somehow timid at this moment.

'And how has it gone?'

'I've really enjoyed it … I've had fantastic sex. Sex that I haven't had in a really long time. Wild sex. To be honest, it's kind of addictive … once you have good sex you just can't leave it behind.'

'And does your partner know you've been seeing escorts?'

'Yes, but not exactly when. So, I've told him I'm seeing escorts, but I won't say when exactly, so he's not at home knowing I'm having sex with a guy.'

'Okay, is he jealous or anything?'

'No. I would say he's relieved. I think he recognised there was something he wasn't fulfilling and now he's glad it's happening somewhere else. We're still happy together. I would say we've never been happier.'

'Okay. And do you see different escorts? How do you book them, what's the process?'

'Yeah, I see different ones, but I do have a favourite. It's mind-blowing sex, and I feel like … I feel like we have a connection. I book them online, I organise the hotel room, and the rest of the details. I feel in control that way. Like

I'm not going to get choked. I'm going to get exactly what I want.'

'And you tell them that?'

'Yes, absolutely. That's the thing … it's transactional, I feel like I'm paying for a service, so I can really ask for what I want, or tell them, that's not working. I never felt like I could say that with my partner, or any other guys.'

'Right, and have you had a lot of sexual partners?'

'No, not really. I've always felt self-conscious about my body, about the scars on my stomach and things not looking right – so I've never felt like … empowered to have sex with guys. When I was younger, I used to go to sex clubs and swingers clubs because I liked the idea of anonymity, not having to build that relationship, just being able to get in and out and have that rush of intimacy.'

'You didn't think you could meet someone out or online and have the same outcome?'

'No. I felt more shy in those situations, and then I guess unable to explore or say what I wanted.'

'Because there was the pretext of a potential relationship, or because they sort of knew you?'

'Both, I guess.'

'Okay, so you mentioned earlier that you see one escort

more than others – are you developing feelings for him?'

She laughs. 'Yeah, I guess a little. It's hard not to – and there's a connection of sorts. I can't explain it. It's like we understand each other.'

'Do you think he feels the same?'

'Yeah, I think so.'

'Do you think you would progress this anywhere? Into a relationship?'

'No, I love my partner. I'm not looking to leave him.'

'Do you think those feelings can co-exist in the same space?'

She pauses and finally says, 'It's hard.'

15

Conclusion: Invisibility

In Carolina Petit's novel, *The Natural History of Love*, Carolina Fonceca is a 16-year-old living on a Brazilian coffee plantation in the mid-1800s. She's trapped in a patriarchal world where her stupid but ambitious brother decides the fortune of all of the family members (following her father's death), and arguably all of those who reside or work on the plantation. Disturbed by his sister Carolina's curious mind and intellect, he removes her from higher education; after all, what use will she be to him if she is clever? In this time, and within this cultural context, no man seeks an intellectual wife – rather a subservient, indolent, pretty one, willing to have many children.

Of course, and thanks to the narrative requirements of a novel (where something has to happen – unlike life, where Carolina simply may have been married off to any suitor and lived a life of silent and terrifying servitude), the Count de Castelnau happens to be brought to their plantation for care after a stint in the Brazilian wilderness, and the two fall passionately in love. He, *apparently*, wants for an educated counterpart. However, in a distressing turn of events reveals he is indeed married in France – and instead takes Carolina on as a pseudo-mistress, proving that it never fairs well for intelligent and ambitious women.

It might be narrative fiction and 1850 Brazil, but what has changed? Some women have been removed from the bonds of servitude (definitely not all). We may have been granted the vote, equal work, and we may have been fed the narrative that we could do everything. But how much has actually changed? Today, we stare down the barrel of other inequities – the gender pay gap (ever widening), and endless care duties (because despite the advent of paternity leave, women are still expected to take on the lion's share of child-rearing responsibilities. In 2022, we're still presented with a situation where the recent 2021 Census demonstrates that women do the majority of domestic duties at home, and in Australia, one woman per week is murdered, or violently assaulted by a man – more often than not, one who was or is an intimate partner.

Although these inequalities don't necessarily speak to the intellect of a woman as an undesirable facet within a relationship, they do speak to the disrespect and the continued subjugation of women. The notion that we are still perceived as less than. That men are somehow our superior, and that we are chattel, to be traded or bartered between men.

My research would demonstrate that a woman who is perceived as 'high maintenance' – whether that be too intellectual, too overdressed, or too difficult – is unwanted. Instead an indolent, subservient, pretty type (as per Brazil, circa 1850, according to Petit's account) is preferred.

Women are still exchanged – from father to husband – when they marry.[44] Women are marked by the name of the father or the husband. They are unable to maintain their identity; instead, they must assume the identity of the man who has conducted the trade and is now proprietor. For those who argue that this is tradition, there is no tradition to it; countries like Italy have legislated against the changing of names via marriage – women must maintain their maiden name, and children are required a double-barrelled surname, where both surnames are included.

Yet we persist with antiquated notions that name changes as a result of marriage are traditional or even more subversively 'romantic' – like the loss of an identity or the submission to a man constitutes some sort of romanticism.

Of course, to argue such points is indeed to be 'high maintenance'. Anyone reading this book might conclude that I'm difficult – perhaps even overly educated. And what happens to an overly educated woman? I await my demise – as described in narrative fiction.

Dating apps subvert this process, they provide women with sexual autonomy, visibility, control of their sexuality. This then has to be squashed by patriarchal forces – like the media, contemporary culture and ideas of the high maintenance woman. The ultimate aim being to make women invisible.

Dating apps present as unsafe and safe places at the same time – particularly for marginalised groups. So, not everyone who uses a dating app is empowered by their usage; many find them to be quite the opposite. Rarely is a queer Asian-Australian man held up as an example by the media of being subjected to 'unsafe' practices on dating apps.

Instead, as demonstrated by the *Four Corners/Hack* piece, white, heterosexual women are generally the group used to illustrate the danger of dating apps. Women who stepped out of the mould, and were more 'visible' were policed by multiple forces: by men on apps who described them as 'high maintenance', and by the media which described them as foolish whores or silly girls.

Although apps like Bumble sought to create environments where women made the first move, they appeared to contemporaneously reinforce ideas that men just can't be trusted. That they are instinctually brutish and toxic; app parameters need to be put in place to interrupt men's propensity to lewd behaviour.

The modern desired woman is expected to be chill, cool, pretty. She is required to simply play along with a heterosexual man's desires, and never be too much. Those of us who want more are simply too difficult, and like Lady Macbeth or Carolina Fonceca – we will meet our inevitable demise.

So, this book marks a standpoint – to women out there,

who are being ever so covertly instructed to smile, play along and make themselves smaller. Invisibility won't save you. Unfortunately, as a woman there is currently no safe space at this point in time; *you will be judged, no matter what.* For being attractive, or not attractive enough. For being too smart, or not smart enough. For being too loud, or too quiet.

There is always *something*.

Of course, there are other narratives and ways of life. Dating apps aren't the only ways people meet other people. White, Western cultures present them as the pinnacle of dating. However, other cultures, sexualities and diverse people have a plethora of other ways to meet and form intimacies. They're not rejected from 'mainstream' dating apps, they reject dating apps! It's just that these stories are never told by contemporary media – who prefer lambasting us all with the same sort of pedestrian narrative.

Women like Celeste exist. They seek out sex workers and different ways of being a woman and living out sexuality. But nobody ever hears about them. They are silenced, among the homogeny of same/same content, which nobody really identifies with.

This is a call to arms to women. To take up as much space

as you like. To be as clever, as madeup, as dull, as vibrant, as curious, or as difficult as you choose.

To live wildly.

To occupy and embrace different spaces.

This is your moment to be, yes, high maintenance.

Embrace it.

Endnotes

1 Bailey, 2012
2 YouGov, 2017
3 Rao, 2011
4 Ling
5 ‹Tinder and how digital dating became a predators' playground' (ABC, 2020).
6 News.com and Mamamia
7 Junkee, 2020)
8 *The Conversation*, 2021
9 BBC, 2021
10 BBC, 2021
11 *The Project*, 5 March 2020
12 described by Dietzel, Myers and Duguay, in *The Conversation*, 2021.
13 Between 5 and 10 March, OkCupid reported a 7 per cent increase in new conversations
14 Portolan, *The Conversation*, 2020
15 active users on Bumble rose by 8 per cent
16 Bumble from 12–22 March, Seattle saw a 23 per cent increase in sent messages, New York City, 23 per cent and San Francisco, 26 per cent.
17 the then CEO of Tinder, Elie Seidman (The Verve, 2020), indicating the rise of an episodic use of dating apps, which coincided with cities going into lockdown
18 OkCupid reported a 188 per cent increase in the number of profiles which mentioned Covid-19

19 My own articles in *The Conversation, The New Daily* and even spots on daytime television
20 Influence of the Kardashian-Jenners on Fourth Wave Feminism by Abbey Rose Maloney— 49
21 Professor of functional and comparative genomics Neil Hall
22 One recent study by Plan International
23 Feminist scholar Akane Kanai draws on the work of Lauren Berlant
24 *Modern Romance,* actor and comedian Aziz Ansari
25 ibid.
26 French feminist and academic Luce Irigaray
27 Jane Austen, *Sense and Sensibility.*
28 ibid.
29 *Pride and Prejudice,* Jane Austen
30 *Labor of Love: The Invention of Dating,* author Moira Weigel
31 Professor Eva Illouz from the Ecole des Hautes Etudes en Sciences Sociales in Paris
32 ibid.
33 Recent research traces the ubiquity of the diamond ring as a symbol of engagement to the discovery of massive diamond mines in South Africa in the late 19th century
34 The Australian wedding industry contributes around $3.6 billion annually to the local economy. There were 56,124 wedding businesses operating in Australia in 2019.
35 According to *Money Smart,* the average wedding costs $36,000 (AUD), and 82 per cent of Aussie singles dip into their savings for their weddings.
36 Sex and the City,
37 Jia Tolentino, *The New Yorker*
38 Barbara Risman's gender structure framework
39 ibid.
40 @triplejthehookup, Instagram
41 Journalist Jennifer Wright wrote in 2019 in *Harper's Bazaar*:
42 Professor Eva Illouz from the Ecole des Hautes Etudes en Sciences Sociales in Paris
43 Dr Bronwyn Carlson's research into Aboriginal use of dating apps, it is true of many ethnically diverse and Indigenous groups
44 French feminist and academic Luce Irigaray argued that women were supposed to be exchanged from man to man (father to husband) – she referred to this as the 'legitimate exchange of women'.

About the Author

Lisa Portolan is an author, screenwriter and researcher from Sydney, Australia. Her PhD from Western Sydney University focuses on how and if dating apps have changed intimacy, whether they continue romantic narratives, and if they reinforce or shift heteronormative stereotypes. Lisa is the author of *Happy As* (Echo, 2018), *Pretty Girls* (Big Sky Publishing, 2020) and *The Overthinkers* (Big Sky Publishing, 2021). She is the host of the popular *Slow Love* podcast, where she interviews a variety of people on their experience with intimacy, and the radio segment, Love Life with Lisa. She is a regular contributor to a variety of Australian publications, and is often featured on television discussing all things love.

Website: www.lisaportolanwrites.com
Twitter: @Lisaportolan
Instagram: @lisaportolan
LinkedIn: Lisa Portolan